White Ignorance and Complicit Responsibility

Philosophy of Race

The Philosophy of Race book series publishes interdisciplinary projects that center upon the concept of race, a concept that continues to have very profound contemporary implications. Philosophers and other scholars, more generally, are strongly encouraged to submit book projects that seriously address race and the process of racialization as a deeply embodied, existential, political, social, and historical phenomenon. The series is open to examine monographs, edited collections, and revised dissertations that critically engage the concept of race from multiple perspectives: sociopolitical, feminist, existential, phenomenological, theological, and historical.

Recent Titles in the Series

White Ignorance and Complicit Responsibility: Transforming Collective Harm Beyond the Punishment Paradigm, by Eva Boodman

Iranian Identity, American Experience: Philosophical Reflections on Race, Rights, Capabilities, and Oppression, by Roksana Alavi

The Weight of Whiteness: A Feminist Engagement with Privilege, Race, and Ignorance, by Alison Bailey

The Logic of Racial Practice: Explorations in the Habituation of Racism, edited by Brock Bahler

Hip-Hop as Philosophical Text and Testimony: Can I Get a Witness?, by Lissa Skitolsky

The Blackness of Black: Key Concepts in Critical Discourse, by William David Hart

White Ignorance and Complicit Responsibility

Transforming Collective Harm beyond the Punishment Paradigm

Eva Boodman

LEXINGTON BOOKS
Lanham • Boulder • New York • London

Published by Lexington Books
An imprint of The Rowman & Littlefield Publishing Group, Inc.
4501 Forbes Boulevard, Suite 200, Lanham, Maryland 20706

www.rowman.com

86-90 Paul Street, London EC2A 4NE

British Library Cataloguing in Publication Information Available

Library of Congress Cataloging-in-Publication Data

Names: Boodman, Eva, author.
Title: White ignorance and complicit responsibility : transforming collective harm beyond the punishment paradigm / Eva Boodman.
Description: Lanham : Lexington Books, [2022] | Series: Philosophy of race | Includes bibliographical references and index.
Identifiers: LCCN 2021044201 (print) | LCCN 2021044202 (ebook) | ISBN 9781793639011 (cloth) | ISBN 9781793639035 (paperback) |ISBN 9781793639028 (ebook)
Subjects: LCSH: Whites--Race identity--United States. | Race awareness--United States. | Racism--United States. | Ignorance (Theory of knowledge) | Responsibility--United States. | United States--Race relations.
Classification: LCC E184.A1 B5983 2021 (print) | LCC E184.A1 (ebook) | DDC 305.800973--dc23/eng/20211020
LC record available at https://lccn.loc.gov/2021044201
LC ebook record available at https://lccn.loc.gov/2021044202

Contents

Acknowledgments

I am grateful for and humbled by the support, guidance, and encouragement I received as this book came into being. I would first like to thank everyone at Lexington Books who worked with me to bring this project to completion. I'm especially thankful to George Yancy for his enthusiasm and belief in this project, and to Jana Hodges-Kluck for guiding me through the process. I'm grateful for their care in managing the project, and for the constructive, clarifying comments I received from an anonymous peer reviewer. Craig Willse provided crucial guidance and feedback in the final stages of the writing process; this book would not be what it is without his encouragement and insight. Their contributions have made this a better book.

I'm grateful to Eduardo Mendieta, Linda Martín Alcoff, Anne O'Byrne, Harvey Cormier, Alan Kim, and other members of the Stony Brook community for their guidance and support when this project was in its very beginnings. I owe special thanks to Eduardo and Linda for their ongoing intellectual and professional support. I'm extremely lucky to have benefited from their direction and good questions, and I continue to be inspired by their commitment to liberatory thinking. I thank them for showing me that philosophy can and should do political work.

The writing of this book benefited from the material support of the Fonds de recherche du Québec and Public Humanities New York, and from the support of my department and college at Rowan University. I'm grateful to my colleagues for supporting me and my research, and to my students for everything they teach me.

I owe many of the questions and framings of this book to those I worked with and learned from in Release Aging People in Prison, the Tzedek Lab, Jewish Voice for Peace, and Marilyn Buck Solidarity Organization/ Third World Peoples' Alliance. Conversations and interactions with members of these groups—Mujahid Farid, Laura Whitehorn, Susie Day, René Valdez, Tony "Al" Simon, Dave George, Michelle Lewin, Anthony Dixon, Jose Saldana, Amelia Paradise, Marcus Brown, Alyssa Adamson, and many others—have shaped and deepened my analysis and continue to challenge and reorient my thinking. I'm particularly indebted to Mujahid Farid (1949–2018) for constantly emphasizing the importance of the "punishment paradigm," and to members of TWPA/MBSO for deepening my understanding of the colonial, imperial, and international nature of capitalism and white supremacy. I also want to acknowledge my indebtedness to the feminist, decolonial, anti-racist, and anti-imperialist thinkers who came before me, without whom my own work would not be possible. I'm grateful in particular to Linda Martín Alcoff, and to Barbara Applebaum for paving the way by developing the concept of "white complicity pedagogy" and for encouraging me from afar, very early on, to publish on white complicity.

The first to call these chapters a "manuscript" were the members of Sarah Schulman's queer academic writing group. I'm indebted to Sarah Schulman, Shirly Bahar, Ilker Hepkaner, Noa Hazan, and João Nemi Neto for their feedback, and for showing me that my writing could be a book. Faria Chaudhry, Kevin Connell, Heather Davis, Rashmi Viswanathan, Phil Opsasnick, Gretchen Hildebran, Tim Johnston, Oli Stephano, and Krissy Mahan read or listened to early versions of several chapters, and Liz Victor offered important assistance at the prospectus stage.

My deep, heartfelt thanks to my friends for thinking with me, sustaining me, and cheering me on. Nina Pariser, Maya Yampolsky, Wazhmah Osman, Whitney Howell, Rashmi Viswanathan, Francis Estrada, Erica Cardwell, Zhaleh Afshar, Faria Chaudhry, Ella Boureau, Eli Nixon, Socorro Hernandez, Erin Bell, Leah Krauss, Julia Alexeyeva, Javier Gaston-Greenberg, Whitney Cox, Paula Ioanide, Tailli Mugambee, Anna Jacobs, Gretchen Hildebran, Liesbeth Schoonheim, Bethany Or, Nathan Gage, Heather Davis, Alyssa Adamson, Phil Opsasnick, Zoe Aqua, Zoe Guigeno, Mariama Koita and Hassane Wele Diallo: your friendship inspires me and keeps me going. I want to express extra special thanks to Rashmi Viswanathan and Francis Estrada. The earliest versions of several chapters were written in their apartment, and benefited from the support of their friendship, company, and delicious cooking. Rashmi practically deserves her own Acknowledgments page, having accompanied me, and the manuscript, from the beginning to the end of the writing process. I'm extremely grateful for her astute editing, willingness to talk through difficult ideas, care, companionship, and sense of humor.

I'm grateful for the support of my parents, Susan and Martin, and grandmother, Roz, who raised me to love books. I thank my brothers, Carl and Eric, for always being there for me, for making me laugh in a way that only siblings can. I especially want to thank Krissy Mahan for being with me as

I brought this project to completion. Incredibly, she read almost every draft from first to last. Her courage, integrity, positive energy and love of fun were important inspirations during the writing and revision process. I'm grateful to her, too, for her beautiful paper cut interpretation of Jericho Brown's 2019 poem "The Water Lilies," which she created for the cover of this book.

Others whose names are not mentioned here, but who have supported me along the way: I trust that you will know who you are. While the arguments I make in this book are influenced by many credited here and in the pages that follow, any mistakes or missteps are mine alone. However and wherever these ideas land, I hope that they will move the conversation forward.

Introduction

The Contradictions and Possibilities of White Ignorance

One year after the police murder of George Floyd, many across the US are fighting to make conversations about race a violation of their civil rights. Some State lawmakers are seeking an outright ban on "critical race theory"—a term (mis)understood by its critics to denote "identity politics," anti-Americanism, "division," and "hate." Idaho and Tennessee have succeeded in making it illegal. The targeting of critical race theory brings new vocabulary and some new adherents to the long-standing efforts in states like Arizona, Texas, and California to ban ethnic studies on the grounds that it is "discriminatory" and "racist." These efforts, while met with vigorous opposition, have also seen some success, with the 2020 upholding of state law HB2281 by an Arizona judge which prohibits any course that "advocates ethnic solidarity." In Texas, after intense resistance among student and community groups, a law was struck down that would have prevented college students from taking women's studies and ethnic studies courses to fulfill their graduation requirements. The so-called "debates" about ethnic studies prepared the ground for the veritable onslaught of attacks on critical race theory in the last year, that included Trump's whitewashing 1776 Commission and efforts to make education and training on race and diversity ineligible for federal funds, mainstream think pieces on the threat of critical race theory to democracy, and countless op-eds and interviews with white parents "concerned" that their children's education was being "hijacked" by the unpatriotic left, ruining their supposedly neutral curricula with toxic indoctrination.

Taken on its own terms, critical race theory refers to the work of activists and scholars interested in studying and transforming the relationships between race, racism, and power.[1] The movement has its origins in the contributions of critical legal scholars like Kimberlé Crenshaw and Derrick Bell, who sought to expose the ways that patterns of racial domination persist in spite of the de jure equality promised by the civil rights gains of the 1960s.[2] While the critical race approach has expanded far beyond its origins in legal scholarship to include research on policy and the workings of institutions like education, health, immigration, these developments maintain critical race theory's interest in how and why racism is normalized, and its commitment to transformation beyond that normalization. As Linda Alcoff has put it, the goal of critical race theory is to "take civil rights to the next level by rethinking the ideas and practices undergirding current conceptions of justice. This requires discerning and unraveling the material and ideological effects of slavery, colonialism, land annexation, and genocide that are still with us in our institutions, our ideas, and our lives."[3] Critical race theory, in other words, identifies patterns of dispossession and domination, and seeks redress for persistent historic and collective wrongs. While the approach is already several decades old, the timing of its negative portrayal is easy enough to understand. The attack on critical race theory—or at least the bogeyman it has been made into by its liberal, conservative, and far right opponents—is a well-funded, defensive backlash in response to the racial justice uprisings of the summer of 2020.[4] Ironically, the current anti-critical race theory movement frames even optional education about race and racism as a violation of "free speech," rather than its opposite: censorship.

What is behind this seeming irrationality is white ignorance, a defensive "non-knowing that is not contingent, but in which race—white racism and/or white racial domination and their ramifications—plays a crucial causal role."[5] Those who would like to make critical race theory and ethnic studies illegal would like to do precisely because these fields make the historical and ongoing dynamics of racism, white supremacy, and colonialism relevant—indeed, essential—objects of inquiry for making sense of our reality. As a California opponent of the controversial, and newly adopted high school ethnic studies curriculum put it, "I'm concerned about critical race theory being the underlying pedagogy when its underlying philosophy is that one group is oppressing another. When students are told that the privileges that they have are all based on race that make them dominant or oppressors over other people, that's a discriminatory practice. It pits groups against each other and is going to create hostility and tensions."[6]

The concept of white ignorance is helpful for understanding why someone might view the effort to explain observable racial inequalities—the factual result of historical and contemporary racial discrimination—as itself a form of *anti-white* discrimination. When parents and conservative teachers claim that discussing race and racism in the classroom is "biased" or "unsparingly harsh towards whites and capitalism,"[7] what we are observing is white ignorance at work, a special and hegemonic form of racial denial. While the word "ignorance" might suggest a deficiency of information, an "accidental omission or gap in understanding,"[8] philosophers like Alison Bailey, Shannon Sullivan, and Linda Martín Alcoff have shown that white ignorance is not a neutral lack of information, but a substantive set of knowledge practices tied to racial benefit, social position, and identity. In his groundbreaking paper on white ignorance, Charles Mills defines it as a particular epistemology that is also political, moral, and material. White ignorance, according to Mills, is the "white refusal to recognize the long history of structural discrimination that has left whites with the differential resources they have today, and all of its consequent advantages in negotiating opportunity structures."[9] Because white ignorance is "socio-structural"—that is, operating through institutions and collective norms—that refusal might not be entirely self-aware or intentional. Either way, white ignorance isn't simply a passive receptivity to false knowledge or incorrect facts, but an aggressively resistant epistemology that, just like those who oppose critical race theory, fights back against the truth about race.

The reversals, denials, and obfuscations of white ignorance are not limited to reactionary politicians and concerned conservative parents. If white ignorance is "socio-structural," then, like white supremacy, it is a normalized and systematized reality that manifests anywhere that whiteness is, including on left, and even in the practice of anti-racism itself. As Linda Martín Alcoff has put it, because of their dominant status in society, white people have a "positive interest in 'seeing the world wrongly.'"[10] This is because their social position and experiences might inhibit what they are motivated to recognize, or because dominant social conventions limit access to particular kinds of knowledge. But given the wide availability of information about race and racism, there is likely a more active, if ambiguous, form of distortion going on.

Virulent opposition to anti-racism education is not just ignorance in the colloquial sense. It is not simply a lack of information, or not knowing any better. It is a collective, epistemological *and* extra-epistemological phenomenon involving *actively managed* denial, even if that denial can be pre-conscious or not quite self-aware. That active denial has been described by some as a "need not to know" after James Baldwin, who wrote of US racism, "This is the crime of which I accuse my country and my countrymen and for which neither I nor time nor history will ever forgive them, that they have destroyed and are destroying hundreds of thousands of lives and *do not know it and do not want to know it.*"[11] We can see in Baldwin's quote that white racial cognition and the responsibility that might accompany it are both ambiguous. How can one want to avoid something if one truly does not know it? White ignorance is contradictory in precisely this sense: one knows that one must protect oneself from what one would rather not admit, a state that Christopher Bollas has called "the desire to be innocent of a troubling recognition."[12] White ignorance, in this way, is a form of political complicity, the epistemic dimension of a system that accords undue benefit to white people, while simultaneously saving them the trouble of accounting for it.

This book takes up that question of accountability, asking in what sense white people are responsible for the epistemic practices that perpetuate white domination and benefit. If white ignorance is not just a personal lack of relevant information, but a structural, political phenomenon, that has an impact on the habits and ways of being of ordinary white people (and not just Republican lawmakers or neoconservative think tanks), then it has an ambiguous moral status. Are ordinary white people "to blame" for supporting policies that will harm and further disadvantage non-white people? When my students use racist "culture of poverty" tropes in my class—statements that associate Blackness with learned cultural inferiority—as attempts to show their care for racial justice, or become hostile when the topic of race comes up, should these cognitive and psychic states be described as a lack of correct information? Are they to blame for their dispositions and reactions? Are those who avow anti-racism to blame for "well-meaning" micro-aggressions? Is whiteness itself a blameworthy condition?

These questions are preoccupations that I share to some extent with those opposed to critical race theory (CRT), though our answers differ significantly. CRT opponents reject the approach precisely because of the implications of racial knowledge for responsibility. Indeed, in Idaho's recently passed legislation, educators are prohibited from teaching that "individuals, by virtue of sex, race, ethnicity, religion, color, or national origin, are *responsible for actions committed in the past* by other members of the same sex, race, ethnicity, religion, color, or national origin" (emphasis mine).[13] This law, like the laws and proposals put forward in other states, seeks to absolve students and governments from responsibility for racism by refusing to acknowledge its existence. According to this law, if systemic racism and white supremacy are not discussed, then no one can make white people responsible for what they did not personally cause. This book makes an argument that is diametrically opposed: I argue *for* white responsibility for events, patterns, and structures that were not necessarily caused or intended. I credit these virulent laws, however, with correctly identifying the problem: how can individuals be responsible for what they didn't cause or intend? Surely they cannot be *to blame*? And if they are not to blame, how can they be responsible?

My project in this book is to help readers out of this seeming conundrum by exploring non-punitive frameworks for responding to collective racial harm—frameworks that prioritize the complexity and material impacts of social relations over adjudications of blame. How indeed can we be responsible for the forces that structure our perceptions, cognition, habits, and relationships—forces that affect even our notions of responsibility? I argue that while there is certainly a time and place for blame, and for feelings of guilt and shame, the collective racial harm in which white people necessarily participate by virtue of being white demands a different set of concepts. As the philosopher Hannah Arendt showed in her writings on German complicity, guilt and responsibility are not synonymous. "Where all are guilty," she wrote, "none are responsible."[14] *White Ignorance and Complicit Responsibility* takes Arendt's lead, looking at white ignorance as a form of complicity that demands a model of responsibility that can take its morally ambiguous, collective character into account. The "debates" on CRT—to say nothing of the everyday instances of white ignorance enacted by regular people and institutions—are crying out for such a framework. In denying the ongoing reality of racism, to call the CRT controversies "debates" is itself a form of white ignorance, since racism and white supremacy are empirically observable, and not up for debate. If only CRT opponents would actually read the feminist and critical race authors I cite in this book, they might find their questions answered and worries about blame assuaged. But, as we will see in the chapters that follow, white denial and blame-based moralities go hand in hand, working together to obscure facts about racial benefit and harm.

Much more than resolving questions of guilt and blame, this book is interested in responses to racial harm that move beyond white moral absolution altogether, but only after understanding the important function that it plays in perpetuating white superiority. Understanding responsibility to be synonymous with moral absolution is not only ineffective; it is also a framework with deep roots in colonial Protestant notions of white mastery and affective economies that associate innocence with whiteness and punishability with non-whiteness.[15] The prioritizing of white moral absolution and psychic relief is both a cause and consequence of the racist punishment paradigm at work in US society that criminalizes, surveils, incarcerates, and murders non-white people. In morality and in the law, the punishment paradigm centers white satisfaction and conceptions of safety and comfort, while repressing, suppressing, ignoring, or maligning non-white movements and non-white political resistance. Understanding a quest for moral absolution as the only defensible response to racial harm is not only unrealistic; it reinforces the tendency for white people to use racism, and the landscape of race in general, to maintain moral and economic standing. This is a crucial analysis for developing white accountability for participation in racial harm that doesn't simply reproduce it by aiming primarily to be a "good white," rather than to transform the conditions that allow for racial harm and white moral capital to occur.

While this book does not offer a program or set of "best practices" for white anti-racism, it does make the case for a philosophical approach: complicit responsibility. This is not a definitive or exhaustive approach, but a contribution to the growing literature on anti-racism and whiteness which I hope will inspire readers to recognize possibilities for accountability beyond white colonial benevolence, saviorism, and vanguardism, all of which reproduce white dominance. So often, the dismay, anger, and anguish that white people feel in response to discovering their participation in structural racism propels them to take up positions of anti-racist visibility and authority in order to assuage these feelings—or it results in isolation and paralysis. These feelings are legitimate and should not be dismissed. But, as transformative justice practitioner Mariame Kaba writes, transformative anti-racist work is "not about your feelings," or "emotional satisfaction."[16] This is not to deny the power of emotion, but rather to emphasize the importance of a different kind of accountability, rooted in complicity, that orients itself around non-white self-determination, leadership, and flourishing, and movements that seek to end racial-capitalism and all its expressions of violence. This is also not to deny the messy, failure-prone reality of white attempts to get beyond white feelings and propensities to want to be visibly "good."

One of the assumptions of complicit responsibility is that whiteness necessarily benefits from relations of domination, capitalist expropriation, colonialism, and imperialism that are not in the past, but ongoing. Races are frameworks that help us to make sense of ourselves and our world, while also being tied to our current set of material conditions. As Paula Moya has written, racial identities are both ascriptive and subjective, a dialectical relationship between our place and role within a set of power structures, and the collective meaning-making and organizing we do in connection to that role.[17] The implication of this dialectical double truth is not that individuals should disavow whiteness by "unbecoming white": racial identities cannot be chosen or unchosen at will. Race is a flexible, historically constructed political position that can be changed, but not by individuals acting on their own. Rather, the implication is to collectively take up the contradictions of white complicity in order to desupremicize whiteness. In the remainder of this introduction, I take up some of the contradictions of whiteness in order to set up the work of the book. I frame the contradictions as questions to emphasize their dialectical tensions and ambiguities. By asking (1) whether white ignorance is willful, (2) whether white ignorance is determined or transformable, (3) whether whiteness should be abolished, (4) whether white anti-racism re-centers white agency, and (5) whether white supremacy is benefitting or killing white people, I intend to show that whiteness is a place of dialectical possibility precisely because of its complicity.

IS WHITE IGNORANCE "WILLFUL"?

White ignorance is a kind of obliviousness about the role of race, enabled by race; it is a hegemonic form of denial that resists the roles played by race and racism and their accompanying benefits. To call it "self-deception" isn't quite accurate, since self-deception involves false belief, and the defensive character of white ignorance indicates that one knows that something must remain unacknowledged. White ignorance is theorized as not as innocent obliviousness, but as an urgent, organized, institutionalized need to protect an identity of moral goodness in contradistinction to its opposite, badness. In *Notes of a Native Son*, Baldwin alludes to the way that racial dichotomies are mapped onto moral ones. "I do not think it is . . . too much to suggest," he writes,

> that the American vision of the world—which allows so little reality generally speaking, for any of the darker forces in human life, which tends until today to paint moral issues in black and white—owes a great deal to the battle waged by Americans to maintain between themselves and black men [*sic*] a human separation which could not be bridged.[18]

Whiteness needs not to know, since truly knowing might dissolve the racial and moral binaries that whiteness has constructed in order to maintain the fiction of its exceptional status. It is in this sense that white ignorance is, as Charles Mills writes, not "merely ignorance of facts *with* moral implications but moral non-knowings, incorrect judgments about the rights and wrongs of moral situations themselves."[19] While these incorrect judgments can sometimes be so egregious that their sincerity can rightfully be doubted, most often, and most perniciously, white ignorance manifests as what Joe Feagin and Henan Vera describe as "sincere fictions" or "personal ideological constructions that reproduce social mythologies at the individual level," thereby functioning to protect white people from having to recognize their own racism.[20]

But if such fictions are "sincere," are they willful? Are the delusions of white innocence and exceptionalism passive absorptions of ideology and messages from the surrounding world, a kind of brainwashing? Are white people dupes, victims of the media or the 1 percent? This framing gets at the contradictory nature of responsibility for white ignorance. While it would be incorrect to ignore the role of school curricula in inculcating students with racist, exceptionalist, ideas about white people, the role of the media and political discourse in reinforcing structural racism through dog whistle politics, and the impact that the repression and concealment of people of color movements for liberation has had on collective self-understanding, none of these alone can explain the persistence of white ignorance. For this reason, many philosophers of white ignorance understand there to be an active dimension to white ignorance, connected to the white investment in maintaining material and psychic benefit.

Feminist philosophers like Vivian May, Linda Alcoff, Peggy McIntosh and Barbara Applebaum have all echoed Marilyn Frye in the view that white ignorance is not passive, but actively willed precisely on account of the benefits derived from it. Frye calls white ignorance "willful" in the sense that "not knowing requires an active interest in ignoring or a resistance to knowing what is right in front of you. White people . . . actively refuse to pay attention to their complicity in racism."[21] These authors argue that this form of ignorance is not only an *active* exertion of structural advantage; they attribute that exertion of advantage to particular ways of being which are also active rather than passive. In *Revealing Whiteness*, for example, Shannon Sullivan rejects the view that racism is the result of "lack of activity and the absence of efforts to seek out information about non-white people and worlds."[22] Sullivan is critical of this view both because it obscures the structural causes of racism and the benefits that it confers on white people, and because it displaces political responsibility by taking racism to be a "merely epistemological" problem, resolvable through knowledge-acquisition.[23] Sullivan characterizes the naive view that racism is passive in the following way:

> Racism is not the product of anything that white people actually do, so the story goes. It is not something that they consciously intend. They might be chided a bit for not rectifying their ignorance of the lives of people of color and the latest scientific advances, but only if they are aware of their ignorance in the first place—for how can people be held responsible for something they did not know about? Blithely wrapped up in a white world, white people often do not see their own ignorance and cannot be faulted for not addressing it, so it seems. Point it out to them, give them accurate information about science and non-white people, and white people will gladly fill in the gaps in their knowledge and eliminate their racism.[24]

Sullivan takes this view to diminish and "soften" the realities of white domination by taking the solution to be rational argumentation and the transparent distribution of information to fill the gaps where important knowledge is missing. She raises the question of responsibility for structural forms of ignorance by calling attention to the *active* verb "to ignore" at the root of the word "ignorance" so that it cannot be thought of as something merely accidental, inadvertent or unintended and easily eliminated.[25]

Sullivan's work shows that white ignorance is part of a set of habits that are "active" engagements that both limit and enable, providing "the means by which one is able to act in the world, and in so doing also [excluding] other possible styles of acting."[26] These habits are "both intimately close because they constitute the self, and elusively distant because of their ability to evade and obstruct conscious attention. They are both the means for change and that which actively interferes with it."[27] The fact that white ignorance is actively willed indicates that it can be changed, that white people can change their habits and themselves. This means that there is possibility in the contradictory status of white ignorant agency: it is shot through with power dynamics, but not manipulated through and through. White people can, on this view, be otherwise.

This doesn't diminish the fact that white ignorance does have a pre-or semi-conscious dimension. The habits of white ignorance, while in a sense active, are often not conscious, self-aware calculations of benefit, but unconscious adaptations to systems constructed to perpetuate white comfort, moral standing, and wealth.[28] While habits certainly are "active" in the sense that they are daily, repeated ways of being, we do not need to understand them as "willed" in order to hold agents responsible for them, nor do we need to understand "willing" as an activity undertaken by atomized rational individuals, uninfluenced by their relationships, experiences, and social contexts. As Helen Ngo shows in *The Habits of Racism*, racism is the process by which bodies are signified through habituation—the ongoing repetitive performance of embodied acts in time and space.[29] These habits support, and are supported by, political, material, and institutional incentives which are simultaneously concealed by the normalization of those habits. While the habits of whiteness do serve to perpetuate schemes of white material and moral capital, and are active in the sense that they involve "activities" and ways of being, they are most often not self-transparent. Rather, some habits of whiteness might seem to have no relation to race, while others are attached to emotional states like "safety," "fear," "threat," and "comfort," that have strong racial associations but that again, might not be self-transparently cultivated.

Without becoming embroiled in debates about the nature of the will, we can accept that white ignorance is an actively perpetuated state, even if those activities are not always consciously intended. As Sara Ahmed writes in her rejection of the idea that institutional racism is something institutions "fail" or "do not" do, "we might want to consider racism as a form of doing or even a field of positive action, rather than a form of inaction."[30] Whether it is an act of will or "sincerely" unintended, white ignorance is still an active set of habits by which white knowers "immunize themselves" to the kind of criticism that might correct their misunderstandings.[31] The classical liberal notion of personal responsibility and rational autonomy so beloved by critics of CRT cannot account for forms of agency that are simultaneously willful, ideologically influenced, and self-obscuring. The complicit responsibility framework advanced in this book accepts that contradictory state of white agency as the starting place for white anti-racist responsibility.

IS WHITENESS DETERMINED, OR TRANSFORMABLE?

While the notion that race is a "social construction" has gained currency in the last few decades, the concept is easily misunderstood to mean that race is an illusion. For liberals and those on the left, this can be difficult to reconcile with the idea of an abstract "system" of white supremacy that accords privilege to those who are white. How can something be illusory, while also seeming so deterministic? But social construction does not make race fictitious or unreal—we take money to be very real, with real world, material consequences, and yet it is also a social construction. While it would take a great deal of social upheaval to eliminate "money" as a set of physical and conceptual objects, this eventuality is not completely impossible to imagine. We might not see money eliminated in our lifetimes, but in no way is money, and the relationships and forms of oppression it engenders, a preordained fact. Money, like most social constructions, is contingent; other means of production and exchange, like barter and gift economies, existed before money, and continue to exist alongside it. The advent of money as a system and set of objects developed as a result of the complex relationship between material circumstances and collective human actions, not because it was preordained or a law of nature. Whiteness, and racial categories in general, are similar in this respect (though evidently not in others!). Racial categories will continue to be relevant, socially meaningful categories that help us interpret ourselves and the world for some time to come. But they are not "natural"—there is no biological basis for race—and, in the same way that their meanings were made through material conditions and relations of production, they can be remade.

As Linda Alcoff has written in *The Future of Whiteness*, we cannot change the fact that whiteness was forged by imperialism, colonialism, European racialism, slavery, and the ongoing dynamics to which they gave rise. But the future of whiteness is not predetermined. While pessimism may be in order about the future of whiteness, "fatalism is not. Fatalism presumes an essentialist take on the meanings of white identity, stripping it of its context of use and removing it from the flows of history."[32] The fact of "social construction" does not mean that whiteness and white supremacy can never be dismantled, that race and racism are natural and inevitable. They are not. As chapters 1 and 2 will show, whiteness and the manifestations of white supremacy are historicizable—tied to the collective actions of human beings in relationship to the possibilities and contradictions of their circumstances. The implication of this is that whiteness—and white supremacy—are not immutable, unchangeable "essences," but real social phenomena tied to the way things are changing in the world and our lives. This means that anti-racism that limits itself to cultivating "awareness of white privilege" for individuals may not have much of an impact. Understanding races as both socially constructed and real means that anti-racism should look to the concrete processes that structure our realities—neoliberal capitalism, imperialism, colonialism—and not just our attitudes, to address racism.

SHOULD WHITENESS BE ABOLISHED?

The connection between whiteness, capitalism, colonialism, and imperialism has caused some on the left to advocate for the elimination of whiteness, a position that some philosophers have called "eliminativism."[33] While the temptations of eliminationism are evident, they lead white people to some particularly bad behavior that has the effect of reproducing white ignorance rather than addressing racist conditions. Famous examples include attempts on the left and the right to "be less white," or to not be white at all, as in the case of Rachel Dolezal, a white woman who claimed to be Black, and in the case of nativists in the US and in my home province of Quebec who claim distant non-white "Indigeneity" as a means of establishing their entitlement to land.[34] The language of being a "race traitor" is less appropriative, and more helpful, as a kind of short-hand for being a traitor to white supremacy culture and institutions. But even that language misleadingly suggests that individual white people can disavow their whiteness—indeed, that anti-racist responsibility *requires* racial disavowal. As the title of this book suggests, I think that this is a misguided approach. Whiteness is an element of our material conditions, the product of systems, norms, laws, and relationships of power. White supremacy can and should be resisted. But individuals cannot abolish it on their own any more than they can abolish capitalism on their own. In fact, ending racial-capitalism as we know it is likely one of the conditions for ending white supremacy.

I believe that this view is implied in the work of authors like James Baldwin and Ta-Nehisi Coates, when they describe white people as those who "think they are white" or who "believe themselves to be white."[35] These formulations are synecdochic insofar as they refer to whiteness as a constructed collective reality. As Baldwin writes in "On Being White . . . and Other Lies,"

> Because they think they are white, they do not dare confront the ravage and the lie of their history. Because they think they are white, they cannot allow themselves to be tormented by the suspicion that all men are brothers. Because

> they think they are white, they are looking for, or bombing into existence, stable populations, cheerful natives and cheap labor. Because they think they are white, they believe, as even no child believes, in the dream of safety.[36]

Insofar as it is a political construction, whiteness is a "lie" of sorts. Individual white people can choose to relate differently to their whiteness. They cannot, however, erase the connection—the connection their whiteness has—to the colonization, militarism, exploitation, exceptionalism, and entitlement that Baldwin describes. Learning about the atrocities undertaken in the name of whiteness, that in turn shaped its definition, is enough to make one want to disavow it. But disavowing one's whiteness is its own kind of lie, and, as we will see in chapter 2, an established trope of contemporary white ignorance. Instead of attempting to transcend whiteness and its attendant responsibilities, I argue that an acceptance of one's whiteness and white complicity is an important condition of white responsibility. Recognizing and accepting the fact of white benefit and participation in harm is the place where collective accountability begins. Facing complicity is the condition of possibility for responsibility.

DOES WHITE ANTI-RACISM RE-CENTER WHITE AGENCY?

Because white ignorance is structural—a collective epistemology connected to politics and histories of domination, colonialism, and exploitation that sets white people up to "see the world wrongly"—it is almost certain to manifest in white efforts to be accountable. We can see this in the way that academia and the non-profit sector compensate white people for engaging in anti-racism or race-relevant topics as a way to signal institutional accountability, without having to make significant changes in institutional culture or practice, or in the ways that white people take up leadership positions in movement and activist settings. Universities and corporations will, for example, invest in "representing representation" by hiring faculty of color, without changing the rules and aspects of the promotion process that actively alienate and exclude non-white people. The outcome is, of course, a high attrition rate, which only compounds a low hiring rate for faculty of color in higher education and other areas, while white people with anti-racist or race-related research agendas will be rewarded with recognition, tenure, or highly paid consulting positions.[37]

Even more pernicious is the way that white participation in social movements is selectively rewarded and credentialed by granting institutions, providing salaries, resources, and recognition to anti-racist white people who are positioned to become invested materially and emotionally in those rewards. White people whose livelihood depends on government and private grants for social justice work may do work that makes a difference in the lives of some, but will be less likely to fight for a world where that work—and the grants and non-profit positions that support it—is not needed.[38] This is not to say that white people should always avoid grants and non-profit work, but rather to draw attention to the traps of white responsibility for anti-racism, which risks occupying a role that perpetuates white reward and dominance even as it also attempts to work against it.

The reach and depth of white supremacy means that, as I show in chapter 3, our very cultures of responsibility and accountability, and the institutions and methods we have set up to carry them out, are not immune. This is what has been called the "double bind of whiteness": the fact that efforts to release oneself from whiteness make one all the more white. White anti-racism involves this kind of double bind, in that white involvement may be both sincere and performative, both effective and self-serving, both motivated by guilt and shame and materially supportive of non-white struggles and initiatives. As I argue in this book, there is no pure, un-complicit white anti-racism as long as white supremacy exists. This is why the goals and methods of anti-racism should be determined by non-white people. For that reason, white anti-racist efforts will necessarily exist in the contradictory space between white initiative and the dismantling of white moral and political authority. Beyond the sometimes navel-gazing and hand-wringing fatalism of whiteness studies, a focus on complicity and complicit responsibility intends to bring whiteness into a dialectical space, where its own implication and position in racist systems can help dismantle them from the inside. As chapter 4 discusses, complicit responsibility takes for granted that anti-racism will always be a dynamic, dialectical process.

IS WHITE SUPREMACY BENEFITTING WHITE PEOPLE, OR KILLING WHITE PEOPLE?

In the wake of Trump's presidency, some have argued that the benefits of whiteness aren't what they used to be, and in some respects, they are right. The austerity, community divestment, and deregulation of neoliberalism have lowered the material "wages of whiteness," creating the resentment and aggrievement that helped Donald Trump become president. The poverty and suffering caused by these developments for people of all races should not be minimized, though we should not interpret it as an indication that white supremacy is over, and that "working class" (read: white) people are the truest victims—a trope promulgated by the right (and sometimes the white left).

What this indicates is that white "benefit" can come in different forms, not all of them merely material. The chapters of this book are committed to outlining those non-material benefits.

What has been framed as "working class white people voting against their own interests" is a fixation among political scientists, with many claiming either that this constructed category of people are "duped" by elites (a discourse that reinforces right-wing populism[39]), or "left behind."[40] Both of these analyses use the designation "working class" problematically, uncritically employing a Reaganist racial construction that includes many middle class people, and neither of these analyses captures the rational self-interest at work when white people vote to defund public goods like education and health care. Even if these policies might seem to be "against their interests," they are expressions of the tenacity of white psychological, psychic, and political benefit—what Du Bois called the "psychic wages of whiteness." Faced with the neoliberal shrinking of the material wages of whiteness, the 57 percent of white people who voted for white nationalism can be said to have been protecting their psychic wage.

The benefits of a form of political status and belonging that ensure never having to be the "mudsill" of society—its lowest rung—should not be underestimated.[41] Nonetheless, there is something to the claim that whiteness is in many ways bad for white people. As Jonathan Metzl shows in *Dying of Whiteness*, racist reluctance to expand the scope of public goods like Medicaid is literally killing white people. On his argument, white supremacy is not benefitting white people, but causing them to deprive themselves of basic services they need to survive.[42] Heather McGhee has made a similar argument, that racism is a "poison first consumed by its concoctors"[43] that drives white people to "drain the pool"—to deprive society and themselves of "nice things" out of a feeling of racial threat. As she writes,

> What's clearer in our time of growing inequality is that the economic benefit of the racial bargain is shrinking for all but the richest. The logic that launched the zero-sum paradigm—I will profit at your expense—is no longer sparing millions of white Americans from the degradations of American economic life as people of color have always known it.[44]

Crucially, however, even if white people have suffered as the "collateral damage" of the war on drugs, police violence, environmental racism, and the gutting of benefits programs, they still have disproportionate access to wealth, property, assets, and safety from state violence. If great numbers of white people will defend their psychological "wage" even at the expense of their health and material gain, but still hold 13 times the median income of

Black people, and feel "left behind" in spite of dominating nearly every area of US life, can we really say that white people are "dying of whiteness"?

Psychologists talk about the "psychological costs" of racism for white people, documenting the shame, isolation, stress, and frustration that white people endure because of their own racism, and the racism of the world around them. Decolonial theorists Frantz Fanon and Aimé Césaire both characterize the position of the oppressor as pathological, a kind of mental illness that warps the humanity of white people. Colonialism, according to Césaire, uncivilizes the colonizers.[45] While it is indubitably true that racism does have a dehumanizing impact on white people, this emphasis can distort the perspective and encourage white aggrievement by overshadowing the non-white experiences and demands that should be at the center of our conversations about racism. To center non-white self-determination and well-being is not a dogmatic principle or a matter of mere representation. To focus on the shrinking of white "wages" also ignores the fact that, as Du Bois' writings show us, white workers' increasing access to public goods "at home" could only take place as a result of increased war and colonial and imperial extractivism "abroad."[46] On a global scale, the entitlements of white workers—whether they are construed as cheap goods, low taxes, or socialized public benefits and services—depend on the exploitation of racialized, colonized people around the world. As important as it is not to diminish the hardships of poor white people, it is also important to recognize that position as one of relative benefit in an international context structured by racial capitalism and imperialism.

White benefit raises the important and difficult question of white motivation. If white anti-racism is problematic and self-centering when it is motivated by guilt, shame, and a desire for moral absolution, should white anti-racism be motivated by benefit and self-interest? This approach to white anti-racism that frames white participation in terms of white spiritual, moral, and even material gain it will deliver has always rubbed me the wrong way, however. The history of white supremacy is driven by white individualistic self-interest, and using that rationale to motivate anti-racism seems to me to be perhaps *too* complicit. In my view, to adopt transactional models of responsibility that compel white people to engage in anti-racism for their own moral, spiritual, or material gain walk a dangerous line, risking the reproduction of white self-centering and entitlement, and the abandonment of movement work as soon as these benefits cease to be forthcoming.

At the same time, white people should see a just world and the remaking of social conditions as good for themselves—though this requires a redefinition of benefit outside a capitalist paradigm of individual reward. Indeed, this may be the only way around the problem of colonial benevolence and white saviorism, as captured by Indigenous Australian activist Lilla Watson's oft-cited adage, "If you've come to help me, you are wasting your time. But if you have come because your liberation is bound up with mine, then let us work together."[47] [48] But white conceptions of liberation are perhaps not the most trustworthy. As Kwame Ture and Charles Hamilton write,

> The whole question of race is one that America would much rather not face honestly and squarely. To some, it is embarrassing; to others, it is inconvenient; to still others, it is confusing. But for black Americans, to know it and tell it like it is and then to act on that knowledge should be neither embarrassing nor inconvenient nor confusing. Those responses are luxuries for people with time to spare, who feel no particular sense of urgency about the need to solve certain serious social problems. Black people in America have no time to play nice, polite parlor games—especially when the lives of their children are at stake. Some white Americans can afford to speak softly, tread lightly, employ the soft-sell and put-off (or is it put-down?). They own the society. For black people to adopt their methods of relieving our oppression is ludicrous. We blacks must respond in our own way, on our own terms, in a manner which fits our temperaments. The definitions of ourselves, the roles we pursue, the goals we seek are our responsibility.[49]

It is only logical that racialized people should determine the shape, form, and method of anti-racist organizing. Hamilton and Ture are clear, however, that white people do have an essential role to play as educators, organizers, and supporters. But taking up this supportive role requires its own active work to decenter white moral standing and forego racial benefit—or use it—in the service of non-white self-determination. If we are going to talk about white liberation, it must be discussed as a complex, relational, coalitional, and dialectical process of rehumanization.

While a world without racial capitalism would improve the conditions of white people's lives, white people's motivation should be to rehumanize themselves, treating themselves with enough dignity and respect to recognize the consequences of their punitiveness and individualism on others and not just themselves, and to reorient themselves toward a different way of being. Developing this kind of motivation requires a framework that understands whiteness as changing and changeable, and responsibility as a realistic, complicit process. Being honest about white benefit, loss, aggrievement, harm, and their possibilities for transformation is the project of this book.

I come to these questions and contradictions as a white person with my own first-person experiences of white ignorance and the uncertainty, complicity, and mistakes that accompany it. Many of the manifestations of white ignorance that I document in this book—the defensive flutterings of white talk, sincere yet performative denouncements of racism, actions undertaken to preempt my being labelled as racist, deriving material and psychic benefit and recognition from anti-racist work—are things that I recognize in myself and my own experience. This book could indeed be considered its own example. As Karen Teel has put it "there is something repugnant about a white person, already the recipient of so many unearned advantages, building a career on analyzing white supremacy, even when one intends to move oneself and other white people toward greater awareness and active rejection of whiteness."[50] "I shudder," Teel continues, "when I consider that I live a life of relative luxury while exercising what for me is truly an *option* to try to redress privilege." But to let fear and shame turn into paralysis and fatalism is much worse than imperfect actions to address participation in racial harm. To enact complicit responsibility is to recognize that white anti-racism will necessarily have this morally ambiguous status. To understand white anti-racism as a pure moral state or as a means of restoring white innocence cleansed of moral compromise is precisely what this book aims to reject. If white ignorance is a paradoxical space, this book looks to inhabit its ambiguities, vulnerabilities, and failures as the starting place for desupremicizing whiteness.

CHAPTER OVERVIEW

Contemporary whiteness isn't merely a form of "privilege"; it is also the denials, displacements, and obfuscations that maintain it. Chapter 1 argues that ignorance and denial are not incidental to whiteness, but are constitutive of it, and central to normalizing and maintaining white supremacy. White ignorance, in other words, is structural; as the epistemic dimension of structural racism, it is not only a matter of behavior and bias, but of how those behaviors and biases tacitly and explicitly serve broader political and economic agendas, with each of those registers supporting the other. Chapter 1 shows that ignorance and denial are what tie seemingly race-neutral liberal racism to right-wing discourses of white loss and aggrievement. By exposing un-knowing, denial, distancing and obfuscation as ingredients in the construction of whiteness as a social and political position that spans ideology and conscious intention, I frame the problem of whiteness as belonging to all of us who can be understood as white.

Chapter 2, "Declarations and Absolutions: Moral Paradoxes of White Ignorance," describes the ways that white ignorance participates in a moral economy centered on white moral absolution that tends to reproduce white moral capital and authority. I trace moralities of white redemption and white saviorism back to strains of early US Protestantism that linked spiritual responsibility to white mastery, arguing that this origin story helps explain some of the specific ways that race continues to be the terrain for establishing white moral standing in settler societies like the US. I find this variety of moral absolution at work in two case studies: "white talk" in the classroom, and institutional declarations of anti-racism. I show that in each case, we can see the traces of white Protestant morality in responses to racial harm that center white agency and moral standing in the project of establishing white innocence.

After showing how white supremacy has warped our very notions of responsibility and accountability by making them synonymous with individual absolution and redemption—a tendency that draws resources and attention away from those most affected by racial harm—chapter 3, "Punitive Whiteness: Affective Economies of White Guilt and Shame," looks at the way that affect contributes to these racialized moral economies. I show how the effects of guilt and shame circulate to establish racialized patterns of belonging, moral worth, and sensitivity on the one hand, and rejection and immutable punishability on the other hand. Rather than rejecting white guilt and shame outright, I outline their ambiguities and limitations. Because guilt and shame are connected to the pre-conscious processes of denial at work in white ignorance, these feelings and dispositions that we tend to associate with responsibility are implicated in the process of racialization. I argue that, while guilt and shame may be galvanizing for some to take anti-racist action, these affects are not separable from a punishment paradigm that took root in the US during the nineteenth century. In this punishment paradigm, guilt, shame, and innocence were, and still are, raced.

Chapter 4, "Complicit Responsibility and Transformative Whiteness," thus argues that the punitiveness of raced moralities demands a different, more accountable orientation toward collective white harm: complicit responsibility. This culminating chapter looks to the tools developed by community accountability and transformative justice practitioners to develop a complicit responsibility framework for white ignorance that begins from the possibility of moral risk, failure, and denial. The complicit responsibility framework is meant to describe a kind of responsibility for participation in collective harm beyond punishment and the quest for white moral absolution. It does so by reframing responsibility and complicity, and outlining some principles that center relationality, non-white self-determination, and coalitional work. Chapter 4 offers a framework that resists the urge to disavow whiteness so that it can participate in the struggle to desupremacize and transform it, complicitly, from within. Taking inspiration from transformative justice as an approach that responds non-punitively to address the conditions of harm, this culminating chapter suggests that "transformative whiteness" can address collective white participation in racial harm while mitigating the saviorist, vanguardist tendencies of white settler moralities.

The chapters in this book are interested in non-punitive white responsibility on the grounds that punitive moralities are closely tied to white supremacy.

My late mentor and teacher Mujahid Farid, the lead organizer of Release Aging People in Prison, would frame mass incarceration as a product of what he called "the punishment paradigm."[51] On his analysis, the punishment paradigm was at the root of mass incarceration, punitive benefits programs and anti-poverty legislation, the school to prison pipeline, the refusal to grant parole to elders after decades behind bars for an act committed in their youth. He saw the punishment paradigm at work in the heartbreaking challenges of reentry, with many returning from prison only to be denied housing, health care, employment, education, and training. Having served thirty-four years in prison himself, he understood all too well that the Board of Parole's obsession with "the nature of the crime" as a reason to deny someone parole for the eleventh or thirteenth time was the product of a framework that did not allow for the possibility of transformation and change. This book is interested in transformative responses to harm that see white attempts to secure innocence as directly related to the institutions that essentialized and racialized Farid's assumed guilt. For that reason, *White Ignorance and Complicit Responsibility* looks to the insights of transformative justice practitioners to begin the process of transformative whiteness—a process that doesn't seek to deny or disavow collective harm, but to change it.

NOTES

1. Richard Delgado, Jean Stefancic, and Foreword Angela Harris, "From Critical Race Theory: An Introduction," in *NYU Press*, 2006, 6.

2. Derrick Bell, *Faces At The Bottom Of The Well: The Permanence Of Racism* (Basic Books, 1992); Kimberle Crenshaw, "Mapping the Margins: Intersectionality, Identity Politics, and Violence against Women of Color," *Stanford Law Review* 43, no. 6 (1991): 1241–99, https://doi.org/10.2307/1229039.

3. Linda Alcoff, "How Critical Race Theory Became The New Conservative Bogeyman," *The Indypendent*, May 25, 2021, https://indypendent.org/2021/05/how-critical-race-theory-became-the-new-conservative-bogeyman/.

4. Isaac Kamola, "Guest Blog: Where Does the Bizarre Hysteria About 'Critical Race Theory' Come From? Follow the Money!" Inside Higher Ed, June 3, 2021, https://www.insidehighered.com/blogs/just-visiting/guest-blog-where-does-bizarre-hysteria-about-%E2%80%98critical-race-theory%E2%80%99-come-follow.

5. Charles W. Mills, "White Ignorance," in *Race and Epistemologies of Ignorance*, ed. Nancy Tuana and Shannon Sullivan (Albany: SUNY Press, 2012), 11–38.

6. John Fensterwald, "A Final Vote, after Many Rewrites, for California's Controversial Ethnic Studies Curriculum," *EdSource*, March 17, 2021, https://edsource.org/2021/a-final-vote-after-many-rewrites-for-californias-controversial-ethnic-studies-curriculum/651338.

7. Ibid.

8. Alison Bailey, "'Strategic Ignorance,'" in *Race and Epistemologies of Ignorance*, ed. Nancy Tuana and Shannon Sullivan (Albany: SUNY Press, 2012), 77–95, 77.

9. Mills, "White Ignorance," 28.

10. Linda Martín Alcoff, "Epistemologies of Ignorance: Three Types," in *Race and Epistemologies of Ignorance*, ed. Nancy Tuana and Shannon Sullivan (Albany: SUNY Press, 2012), 47.

11. James Baldwin, *The Price of the Ticket: Collected Nonfiction, 1948–1985* (Macmillan, 1985), 334.

12. Christopher Bollas, *Being a Character: Psychoanalysis and Self Experience* (Psychology Press, 1993), 167.

13. Caitlin O'Kane, "Nearly a Dozen States Want to Ban Critical Race Theory in Schools," May 20, 2021, https://www.cbsnews.com/news/critical-race-theory-state-bans/.

14. Hannah Arendt, "Collective Responsibility," in *Amor Mundi: Explorations in the Faith and Thought of Hannah Arendt*, ed. S. J. James W. Bernauer, Boston College Studies in Philosophy (Dordrecht: Springer Netherlands, 1987), 43–50, 47.

15. Katharine Gerbner, *Christian Slavery: Conversion and Race in the Protestant Atlantic World* (University of Pennsylvania Press, 2018); Jackie Wang, "Against Innocence," *LIES Feminist Journal* 1, no. 1 (2016), https://www.liesjournal.net/volume1-10-againstinnocence.html.

16. Mariame Kaba, *We Do This 'Til We Free Us: Abolitionist Organizing and Transforming Justice* (Haymarket Books, 2021), 137.

17. Paula M. L. Moya, "What's Identity Got to Do With It? Mobilizing Identities in the Multicultural Classroom," in *Identity Politics Reconsidered*, ed. Linda Martín Alcoff et al., The Future of Minority Studies (New York: Palgrave Macmillan US, 2006), 96–117, https://doi.org/10.1057/9781403983398_7.

18. James Baldwin and Edward P. Jones, *Notes of a Native Son*, 1st edition (Boston: Beacon Press, 2012), 142–43.

19. Mills, "White Ignorance," 22.

20. Joe R. Feagin et al., *White Racism: The Basics* (Psychology Press, 2001), 187.

21. Marilyn Frye, in Barbara Applebaum, *Being White, Being Good: White Complicity, White Moral Responsibility, and Social Justice Pedagogy* (Lexington Books, 2010), 41.

22. Shannon Sullivan, *Revealing Whiteness: The Unconscious Habits of Racial Privilege* (Indiana University Press, 2006), 18.

23. Where epistemology is understood as a theory of knowledge separate from values or interests.

24. Ibid.

25. Ibid., 44.

26. Ibid., 24.

27. Ibid., 44.

28. I say "often" because there are certainly cases where deflection is perfectly conscious.

29. Helen Ngo, *The Habits of Racism: A Phenomenology of Racism and Racialized Embodiment* (Lexington Books, 2017).

30. Sara Ahmed, *On Being Included: Racism and Diversity in Institutional Life* (Duke University Press, 2012), 45.

31. Elizabeth Spelman, "Managing Ignorance," in *Race and Epistemologies of Ignorance*, ed. Nancy Tuana and Shannon Sullivan (Albany: SUNY Press, 2012), 119–31, 119.

32. Linda Martín Alcoff, *The Future of Whiteness* (John Wiley & Sons, 2015), 150.

33. Paul C. Taylor, *Race: A Philosophical Introduction* (John Wiley & Sons, 2013).

34. Daryl Leroux, *Distorted Descent* (Winnipeg: University of Manitoba Press, 2019).

35. Baldwin, James, "On Being 'White'. . . And Other Lies," in *Black On White: Black Writers on What It Means to Be White* (New York: Schocken Books, 1998); Ta-Nehisi Coates, *Between the World and Me* (Spiegel & Grau, 2015).

36. Baldwin, James, "On Being 'White'. . . And Other Lies," 180.

37. "Race, Ethnicity, and Gender of Full-Time Faculty Members at More Than 3,400 Institutions," *The Chronicle of Higher Education*, May 21, 2021, https://www.chronicle.com/article/race-ethnicity-and-gender-of-full-time-faculty-at-more-than-3-700-institutions/.

38. INCITE! Women of Color Against Violence INCITE!, *The Revolution Will Not Be Funded: Beyond the Non-Profit Industrial Complex* (Duke University Press, 2017).

39. Aurelien Mondon and Aaron Winter, *Reactionary Democracy: How Racism and the Populist Far Right Became Mainstream*, 2020.

40. Arlie Russell Hochschild, *Strangers in Their Own Land: Anger and Mourning on the American Right* (New Press, 2016); J. D. Vance, *Hillbilly Elegy: A Memoir of a Family and Culture in Crisis* (HarperCollins, 2018).

41. W. E. B. Du Bois, "Marxism and the Negro Problem: W E B Du Bois. Org," *The Crisis*, 1933.

42. Jonathan M. Metzl, *Dying of Whiteness: How the Politics of Racial Resentment Is Killing America's Heartland* (Basic Books, 2019).

43. Heather McGhee, *The Sum of Us: What Racism Costs Everyone and How We Can Prosper Together* (Random House Publishing Group, 2021), xxi.

44. Ibid.

45. Aimé Césaire, *Discourse on Colonialism* (NYU Press, 2001).

46. W. E. B. Du Bois, "The African Roots of War," *Monthly Review* 24, no. 11 (April 3, 1973): 28, https://doi.org/10.14452/MR-024-11-1973-04_3.

47. Lilla Watson, "Contribution to Change: Cooperation out of Conflict Conference: Celebrating Different, Embracing Equality," https://uniting.church/lilla-watson-let-us-work-together/.

48. Watson is credited with this quote, having used it in a keynote address in 2004, but cites a collective process as its true origin. She prefers the quote to be attributed to "Aboriginal activists in Queensland, 1970s."

49. Charles V. Hamilton and Kwame Ture, *Black Power: Politics of Liberation in America* (Knopf Doubleday Publishing Group, 2011).

50. Karen Teel, "Feeling White, Feeling Good: 'Anti-Racist' White Sensibilities," in *White Self-Criticality beyond Anti-Racism: How Does It Feel to Be a White Problem?*, ed. George Yancy, Reprint edition (Lanham: Lexington Books, 2016), 33.

51. Mujahid Farid and Laura Whitehorn, "Release Aging People in Prison (RAPP): Challenging the Punishment Paradigm," *Socialism and Democracy* 28, no. 3 (September 2, 2014): 199–202.

Chapter 1

White Ignorance Is Structural

In the aftermath of the presidency of Donald J. Trump, whose term ended with the violent storming of the US Capitol by white supremacist groups, the problem of whiteness is difficult to deny. The attack, which took place the day the election results were to be certified, was an organized mobilization of white nationalist and other far right groups to "take the country back" and "stop the steal" of an election fairly won by Democrats Joe Biden and running mate Kamala Harris, the first woman, first African American, and first Asian American to be elected Vice President in US history. While the overwhelmingly white, male mob included members of different right-wing groups with a range of views on the legitimacy of the state, white aggrievement, revanchism, and entitlement were clearly expressed by the mob, driven, as always, by anti-Black racism, anti-Semitism, xenophobia, and anti-democratic sentiment. For these far (and some mainstream) right groups, and the many ordinary white people who participated in the attempted coup, an election won by majority Black and brown cities, that put an historic number of women, Black, Indigenous, and people of color in office, could only have been "stolen" or illegitimate.

White violence in response to even small advances in civil rights for racialized groups, and Black people in particular, is constitutive of US reality. This whitelash to non-white resistance has shaped US laws, land ownership and use, the economy, the criminal justice system, the education system, and has normalized white material, political, and psychic advantage. But as glaringly obvious as that is to those who feel its impact most acutely, the tenaciousness of white power and benefit still bears repeating, and explaining, to those who do not. This chapter addresses the devastating persistence not just of white supremacist acts of terror and revanchism in response to Black and people of color self-determination, but of the everyday forms of distancing, denial, and obfuscation that falsely treat racist terror as exceptional, extreme, or alien to the status quo. The need for more books, more op-eds, more trainings, more webinars on the centuries-old problems of US whiteness and white supremacy indicate a deeper epistemic issue that seems to defy our very definitions of knowledge. That epistemic phenomenon is white ignorance, the collective white resistance to acknowledging the roles played by race and racism and their accompanying benefits. White ignorance is a need not to know that protects whiteness through hegemonic denial. In this chapter, I look at white ignorance in political context, arguing that it can only be understood through the structural role that it plays—that is, the way that white supremacy operates through collective epistemic processes of denial and deflection that serve to maintain patterns of benefit and exploitation. White ignorance is structural, because it is about power as much as it is about knowledge.

To say that white ignorance is structural is not to say that it is inevitable. But to claim, as some commentators have, that the January 6th attack was the "last gasp" or "funeral" of white supremacy, is clearly incorrect, even if it is true that it was a reactionary response to the biggest civil rights mobilization since the 1960s.[1] As strong as the uprisings in response to police murders have been, and as much as the movement for racial justice and accountability has grown, we should not expect white nationalism or the tendencies that brought about the Capitol attack to go away any time soon. This is because white supremacy is not limited to the activities of far right groups and the cult of the 45th president, but is an established political and economic system that operates through norms, laws, and habits that preserve white power and benefit. To the extent that benefit is a feature of whiteness itself, the claims of far right groups and a status quo that preserves racial advantages for regular white people are not opposites, but cut of the same cloth. Without making false equivalences or ignoring the virulence and violence of the far right, we can still say that far right and liberal racism are part of the same set of symbiotic economic and political relationships that work to maintain white benefit across ideological commitments. And when the realities that maintain white entitlement and privilege are challenged, as they are now, whiteness will fight back to preserve its standing—whether or not it is fully conscious or cognizant of doing so. This means that for those of us who are described by the category "white," who benefit from the system of white supremacy, Dwight Boyd's contention that "our mobs are always with us" has never been more evident.[2]

And yet, for those of us who can call ourselves white, denial of "our mobs" persists. Even if many are beginning to grapple with the problem of whiteness for the first time after the events of 2020 and 2021, we can still ask how it could have taken so long for this awareness to set in, given the observable reality of hundreds of years of racial-capitalist exploitation and creative resistance thereto. If the facts are there for all to see and the histories available for all to read, how is it that racial inequality persists, that Black, brown and Indigenous people are poorer, sicker, less educated, more policed, more hurt and killed by the police, more incarcerated, and exposed to more toxic environments than others, and that complex histories of organized resistance to state repression are so often ignored, concealed, or erased? The awkwardness of recent white "discoveries" of centuries of entrenched white supremacy in politics, policy, economics, and collective ways of life indicates that there is an important epistemic dimension to racist systems—a kind of self-concealment and denial by which whiteness protects itself from recognizing its own role. This epistemic limitation is what philosopher Charles Mills has called white ignorance, defining it, as we saw in the introduction, as "a non-knowing that is not contingent, but in which race—white racism and/or white racial domination and their ramifications—plays a crucial causal role."[3] White ignorance is not simply a neutral lack of knowledge, but a racially motivated need not to know that "resists" and "fights back" when challenged, even going so far as to present itself *as* knowledge.[4] [5]

Beyond individuals' emotional fragility in response to questions of race and racism, white ignorance is a form of *collective* denial, managed and perpetuated through norms, laws, ideologies and affective and moral habits, which serve to uphold collective white benefit through its obfuscation. This means that whiteness is not only about "white skin privilege"—about external treatments and benefits accorded to those who are white by third-party arbiters—but also about a group orientation of entitlement to material, moral, intellectual, and emotional comfort and ease and a tendency to defend that entitlement when it is threatened. Contemporary whiteness, then, isn't merely "benefit" or "privilege"; it is also the denials, displacements, and obfuscations that maintain it. Ignorance, in other words, is fundamental to the preservation of whiteness as a category, along with all of its attending benefits. This chapter shows that ignorance and denial are not incidental to whiteness, but are constitutive of it. The reason for this is that whiteness is not simply an identity, but a flexible and constructed social and political position built through exploitation, colonization, appropriation, and violence. Ignorance is central to normalizing and maintaining the power of that construction, not just at the level of individual cognition, but at the level of laws and legal language, collective norms and conceptions, and notions of the right and the good.[6] In that sense, white ignorance is structural; as the epistemic dimension of structural racism, it is not only a matter of behavior and bias, but of how those behaviors and biases tacitly and explicitly serve broader political and economic agendas, with each of those registers supporting the other.

This chapter describes the structural nature of white ignorance in order to explain its perniciousness and durability. In defining white ignorance as a form of collective, normalized and institutionalized denial that perpetuates racial harm by avoiding, obfuscating, and rationalizing its existence, I set up the moral and political problem of taking responsibility for the political circumstances that shape cognition. The work of this chapter is to explain why it is that whiteness manifests as a kind of epistemic limitation. I show that ignorance is a central force in the perpetuation of a racializing system that produces and exploits "group-differentiated vulnerability to premature death" for the benefit of white people.[7] While whiteness and white ignorance do manifest in the behavior of individuals, those psychological tendencies cannot be understood without an understanding of how individual white people participate in broader systems of exploitation and benefit—and maintain the racial denial that holds these systems in place. This first chapter thus shows that ignorance and denial are what tie seemingly race-neutral liberal racism to right-wing discourses of white loss and aggrievement. In this sense, white ignorance is hegemonic.

I begin by defining what whiteness is, and what it isn't. I define whiteness as a site of collective concealment, a political construction rooted in colonial and imperial exploitation which continues to be used for material, emotional, and social benefit. I establish whiteness as a historicizable and flexible category that shifts to accommodate new forms of production and in response to new group interventions. Whiteness is a malleable but objectively real form of power that cuts across class, ideology, and political commitments, while working to normalize its dominance. The second section of the chapter looks at the centrality of denial and deflection in the maintenance of whiteness, characterizing white ignorance as the epistemic dimension of white supremacy. Whiteness and white ignorance persist, I argue, because ignorance and denial are constitutive of whiteness. I show that white ignorance is a form of denial insofar as it isn't merely the absence of knowledge, but an intricate set of defenses meant to protect whiteness from what it cannot admit that it knows. If white ignorance is so persistent, it is because it is a "twilight state" between knowing and not knowing that aggressively deflects responsibility elsewhere, ready to defend itself against the charge of racism. More than passive obliviousness or the ableist-termed "colorblindness," white ignorance is in fact a highly functional form of cognition, "dysfunctional" about the facts of racism, but highly successful in maintaining dominance through the appropriation of racial harm. The third section of this chapter thus argues that aggrievement is a hegemonic expression of whiteness, and that ignorance is crucial for understanding its active reversals and deflections. I show that aggrieved ignorance is the missing piece for understanding how systems and structures perpetuate white benefit. In the final section of the chapter, I show that deflection and aggrievement are at work in the politics of the liberal mainstream. By construing racism as extreme, contemporary liberal discourses like that of "free speech" demonstrate the hegemonic character of white ignorance.

By exposing un-knowing, denial, distancing and obfuscation as ingredients in the construction of whiteness as a social and political position that spans ideology and conscious intention, this chapter frames the problem of whiteness as belonging to all of us who can be understood as white—even if we did not storm the capitol, perpetuate racist conspiracy theories, use racial slurs, or have ancestors who owned and exploited other human beings. The problem of whiteness is rooted in the fact that it is collectively and institutionally maintained, something lived and breathed, a perception-defining and limiting condition. As much as some white people may want to shed it as an identity (and while some do, many do not), whiteness is not something that can be disavowed, even if we can choose our political relationship to it. As Iris Young writes of social positions, we do not choose them; they choose us, making us responsible for "our mobs"—those who are explicitly white supremacist, those who passively accept the status quo, and those who still benefit even in their dogged and deliberate efforts to fight white supremacy.[8] And white supremacy can and should be fought. Whiteness and white supremacy are not natural or inevitable, even if they are vociferously maintained by laws, norms, ideas, and the collective habits of individuals. But in order to resist white supremacy as a system and an ideology, we need to first get clear on what whiteness is, and the role that ignorance plays in maintaining it as a position of social and political advantage.

WHITENESS AS A POLITICAL POSITION

Whiteness is a political construction rooted in colonial and imperial exploitation, which continues to be used to gain collective access to material resources and political, economic, and emotional benefits. It is a flexible, objectively existing form of power that cuts across differences among white people. Whiteness is an observable category, but, as with any racial group, white people are not homogenous and whiteness is not essentializable. To be white has no basis in biology and is not reducible to skin color or to the personal identifications that make meaning of reality on an individual basis. While bodies and their physical features are experienced in a way that is "real," the racial meanings of those features are a product of ideology, culture, and political economy. White people are located within a global system of interlocking forces of domination—imperialism, colonialism, gender and class exploitation—that not only accords them racial benefits, but does so by exploiting the labor, past and present, of those so positioned in relation to them. This kind of political whiteness describes the wealth accumulated by white people as a result of slavery and laws linking whiteness to property in the US, but also to the ways that those of us in the global north exploit the productive and reproductive labor of those in the global south to maintain lifestyles of commodity consumption. That colonial dynamic is at work internally to global north countries like the US, which exploit racialized surplus laborers—migrants, Black people, and other people of color—to grow food and perform care work such as cleaning and elder care for extremely low pay, all on stolen land. In this sense, whiteness under white supremacy is very much about power, production, and reproduction, and whose embodied, emotional/affective, productive, and reproductive labors are exploited for the comfort and profit of others. Whiteness is not only the rationale for these relations of production, but is generated by and through them. This is true on a global scale, and can be observed in the interrelated histories and ongoing dynamics of colonialism and imperialism around the world, from the brutal race-making projects of the British empire in India, North America, and beyond, and of Spain, Portugal, France, and the Netherlands in Central and South America; to the European scramble for Africa in the nineteenth century; and the Euro-American reshaping of the Middle-East in the twentieth century. These examples of racial imperialism are not only manifestations of white European entitlement and material interest, but are material circumstances that had a role in creating the category of whiteness itself. I refer to this aspect of whiteness as "political" precisely because it has to do with the power to create and reinforce patterns of collective benefit and self-determination for white people across the globe. The term "political," too, is broad enough to account for the dynamic relationships between culture and relations of production and social reproduction without reducing race to either.

This is not to say that there can be no authentic cultural identities for those who are able to identify as white. As Linda Alcoff has shown, whiteness is "one and many": a meaningful (if flexible and contextual) category in terms of its historical codification, application, and tendencies, that is also refracted into many cultural and ethnic identities, some of which were not always considered "white."[9] Scholars disagree about whether whiteness can count as a legitimate identity with its own cultural markers, or if it is merely a political position having to do with access to property, wealth, and civil and social belonging paid for through the loss of white ethnic immigrant culture. Some believe that white identity achieved through cultural assimilation is not inherently racist, even if its origins are.[10] Others, like Paula Ioanide and Cheryl Harris, maintain that whiteness has no inherent unifying characteristic aside from its constitutive power to exclude, control, and own[11]—a view shared by proponents of the "white supremacy culture" framework, who take the content of white culture to be associated with the protestant work ethic, moral rectitude and defensiveness, and capitalist productivity.[12] But however we delimit the content and possibilities of whiteness, whatever implications we draw from the story of its construction, it is not fictional but real, with real effects. Whiteness was and is constructed by laws, norms, and group behaviors tied to production, citizenship, ownership, and colonial nation-state-formation, and is, in this sense, a sort of "lie," as James Baldwin put it.[13] As much incoherence as it may take to maintain such a lie, it is one that has been enforced and maintained over hundreds of years, and its effects are much deeper than deception, and far from fictional. Whiteness is more aptly described as a "profound site of concealment" and opacity that operates structurally, despite, and because of, white attempts to dis-identify with it.[14] While whiteness is maintained through a refusal to acknowledge its own role, whiteness itself is a very real social and political phenomenon.

Because whiteness is multidimensional, and multivarious, while also being a historically codified and normalized political position, there is a good deal of public confusion about the definition of whiteness and how white people themselves should contend with it. The possibility of white anti-racism or white anti-racist identity is of particular controversy, since any attempts to transcend whiteness seem to embody the assumptions of mastery and critically self-aware subjectivity that have underwritten white racial formation from the beginning.[15] Among scholars in whiteness studies, much of the disagreement seems to live in the grey area between individual and collective agency. Noel Ignatiev's 1990s journal *Race Traitor*, for example, advocated the process of "unbecoming white" through individuals' rejection of white identification as a form of anti-racist identity—a stance critiqued by Alcoff in *The Future of Whiteness* as individualistic, misguided, and apt to reproduce racist patterns through cultural appropriation and denial of the collective and structural reality of whiteness. Alcoff is right that individual white people cannot simply shed their whiteness by choice in a political and material reality so deeply structured by race and racism. But, as she writes, individuals can indeed make choices about their relationship to their whiteness without disavowing its reality or the structural benefits accrued through it—even if these choices carry no guarantee of success. That is why I focus in this chapter on the political dimension of whiteness, even if emotion, affect, and culture do serve as important channels for white supremacy to be reproduced.

Faced with the seeming abstractness of political whiteness, along with the horrors of racism, the recent demand among white people for self-help-style books is understandable. But psychological framings of whiteness like "white fragility,"[16] and cultural framings like the elements of "white supremacy culture" outlined by activists Kenneth Jones and Tema Okun, while helpful for de-normalizing whiteness and addressing some of its manifestations, can run the risk of essentializing it while de-emphasizing the political and economic forces in which these psychological and cultural patterns of behavior are entangled. While whiteness is not synonymous with material benefit alone, since many white people are also poor, whiteness is the range of non-essential associations with white embodiment that serve to mark the distinction from Blackness and other forms of non-white racialization in a system built for white people to have relative dominance. Even in instances when being white does not involve access to wealth—and historically and statistically it does—whiteness associates bodies identified as white with forms of material advantage like access to work, land, and housing, greater self-determination in labor, and greater physical and emotional safety.

Framings that overemphasize culture and psychology do not get to the root of whiteness as a historically developed social position that has to do with the state, the economy, and access to resources.[17] The function of emotion in maintaining white dominance is undeniable, as Du Bois shows so clearly in his framing of cross-class white allegiances as motivated by the "wages of whiteness."[18] In colluding with the capitalist owning class through implicit and explicit agreements, poor and working class white people were able to benefit from "public and psychological wages" in exchange for ensuring the stability of the social order required for the steady accumulation of capital, largely through the "terrorization and subordination of the [racialized] working class."[19] But to focus only or primarily on psychology and culture also has the impact of making white benefit inevitable, since it is tied to one's assumed essence. As Joel Olsen has written, racial oppression is about power, not merely "cultural conflict."[20] Neither can whiteness be understood as merely about class and class allegiance, since, as historians have shown, racialism and racial prejudice predated the advent of a classed society under capitalism.[21] Ignoring the dynamic political construction of whiteness by attributing it exclusively to either culture or class leads to misguided and decontextualized exhortations in diversity trainings to white people to "be less white,"[22] or to the reduction of lower and middle class white people to mere dupes of the ruling class without agency of their own in perpetuating, benefiting from, and resisting white supremacy. In both cases, white people are left with facile understandings of race and few tools to address the root causes of racism. These reductive and essentializing accounts of whiteness treat it as if it were an incontrovertible personal failing, or a static position, rather than a relational role in a dynamic set of relationships of power.

Whiteness cannot be disavowed by individuals as long as racial-capitalist modes of production and exploitation are in place, but individuals can make choices about their everyday racial allegiances—even if these choices may not result in "successful" anti-racism, and are unlikely to result in any kind of white anti-racist self-mastery. Understanding whiteness as a historicizable and flexible political category is both a more accurate description of the role whiteness can have across class, ethnicity, culture, and ideology, and the role individuals and groups can have in resisting and fighting white supremacy, while accepting the severe epistemic, social, and political limitations posed by whiteness itself. Whiteness does express itself through group behaviors that can be considered "cultural." But its connection to power is more accurately described as a political reality or ontology that understands white ways of being as relationally tied to anti-Blackness and other forms of racial othering and exploitation that perpetuate white advantage in an ever-changing set of circumstances.

That perpetuation of white advantage is about both race and class, while going beyond each of them. Most contemporary theorists of racial-capitalism reject the class-reductionist view that race is "superstructural," and therefore does not have a primary causal role in relations of production, which are thought to be defined by "substructure" alone. The consequence of the class-reductionist position is to view racial prejudice as a mere secondary consequence of the advent of capitalism, and incidental to revolutionary work. The Black radical tradition has taken a more dialectical position. Cedric Robinson showed in *Black Marxism* that capitalism took up pre-existing forms of racial prejudice that date back to Medieval Europe;[23] Gerald Horne has shown in the *Dawning of the Apocalypse* that white supremacy has roots in the use of Christianity as a colonizing force.[24] In this book, I subscribe to the idea that production, ideology, and culture are mutually entangled. Even if we cannot ignore the central importance of "production" broadly understood, class alone cannot explain the persistence and violence of racism. The concept of racial-capitalism can account for this dialectical relationship between culture and relations of production, and the ways that even our notions of class are necessarily raced.

White supremacy does operate on a global scale, but race and racial orders vary according to material conditions. The category "white" as we know it in the US today was originally constructed and shaped by the process of establishing the plantation economy in the eighteenth century, and adapted and adjusted along with industrialization in the global north and the consolidation of the US nation state in the nineteenth and twentieth centuries. While the specific causal relationships between race, racism, capitalism, and settler colonialism and imperialism are contested, their connections are undeniable: one cannot understand contemporary whiteness separately from the advent of capitalism and its processes of primary accumulation.[25] The first codifications of whiteness and Blackness in the US can be found in the eighteenth century in the US, when laws with the purpose of inhibiting multi-racial rebellion against slavery and indentured servitude defined whiteness as unslavery and the ability to own property, including human property, and Blackness as slavery, the inability to own, and the possibility of becoming property. As a response to growing demand for cotton in the industrializing North, Britain and Europe, and the growing frequency of rebellions against working conditions by both enslaved Africans and white workers, the planter class in the US

South established slave codes which made white indentured servants a distinct class and gave them certain privileges and power over those who were not white.[26] This status included the ability to patrol, hunt down, capture, and punish those who were enslaved, and, once fugitive slave laws were put into effect, those who had escaped slavery, and even people of African descent who were born free. This set in motion the ongoing dynamics of the US as a settler colony, with white people continuing into the present in the role of settler colonists with respect to both African and Indigenous people.[27]

Motivated by the imperial triangulation of economic interests of planters in the South and industrialists in the North and Europe, Blackness was legally associated with unfreedom and internal colonization. This manifested as the inability to vote and run for office, own land, learn to read and write, be with one's family and children, participate in civil society, and determine the conditions of one's life, work, and bodily well-being. This legal framework laid the political and material groundwork for the patterns of white entitlement and Black, Indigenous, people of color, and migrant resistance we still see today. It also represents the solidification of an epistemology of reversal and projection where the white European seizure of land, bodies, and labor became the criminalization of Black people and people of color as thieves and murderers; where the mass rape of Black and brown women by white men became the racialized sexual predator; where confining racialized people in "ghettos" and prisons became the result of "cultures of poverty," rather than the product of redlining and consistent exclusion from the benefits of white citizenship.[28]

These reversals are used to justify repression. The inhibition of non-white political participation—as we saw on January 6, 2021, and are continuing to see in recent legislation to curtail voting rights in states like Georgia—is a feature of whiteness as a political position and is tied to its capitalist, accumulative origins. If whiteness is an ongoing allegiance that accords material, emotional, public, and political "wages" to white people, we can see this in the ways that non-white advancement and resistance has been consistently contained and punished, from the crushing of the first Reconstruction by capitalists, lawmakers, and violent Jim Crow militias, to the jailing and policing of anti-racist activists and leftists during the second Reconstruction, to the use of mass incarceration and militarized policing and surveillance to eliminate civil rights activists and the communities they represented—communities made into "surplus" populations as a result of neoliberalization and the rollback of funding for social programs.[29] While these historic reestablishments and adjustments of whiteness do always harm poor and working class white people, they always affect nonwhite people first and worst. Most white people do not understand themselves as engaging in political repression by virtue of being white. But repressive attacks against the self-determination and enfranchisement of Black, Indigenous, and other colonized people, serve to maintain a system that attaches benefits to whiteness, and, by extension, to white people. White ignorance is political because a whiteness that denies the historical construction of its own normativity cannot recognize Black and POC resistance to racism and its role in giving content to the violence of white entitlement.

Looking at the historical trajectory of whiteness as a social and political position, we can see a relational dynamic at work, where the benefits of property ownership, labor rights, political participation, self-defense, enjoyment, and self-determination are understood to be in contradistinction to the racialized non-having of those things. Heather McGhee has called this the "zero sum paradigm," which leads white people to the belief that if their advantages were achieved through violence and exploitation, then non-white advancement will visit these threats on them.[30] Social scientists have found that this viewpoint is prevalent among white Americans, but very rare among non-whites. This shows that white group identity is shaped by an ideology that sees access to power and resources as established in relation to the deprivation of non-white people. As George Yancy has shown, whiteness is embodied, experiential, and "transitive," insofar as "its being presupposes others, signifying a relational constitution that takes place within material history and situational facticity."[31]

To define whiteness as a political, economic, social, and even ontological position rather than as merely appearance, culture, or psychology allows us to make sense of the malleability of whiteness to its circumstances. It allows us to see, for example, that "white ethnics" were not arbitrarily included in the category "white," but were accorded political status in order to bolster white numbers in the US at a time when people of African descent were migrating into northern cities, fleeing the backlash to Reconstruction and then Jim Crow violence. The status "white" was acquired as a means of maintaining what W. E. B. Du Bois and David Roediger have called *Herrenvolk* democracy: a race-based system constructed for the political participation and benefit of a dominant group, and civic exclusion and exploitation of racialized others. It is in this sense that "a white person is a person called white by other whites," as Alain Locke claimed: whiteness as a structural position is defined by the maintenance of its own relational dominance.[32]

The structural nature of whiteness does not mean that all white people are treated the same way, or that they have access to the same material resources; only that in certain instances, differences between white people are subordinated in the interest of a "white solidarity" forged by global patterns of oppression. And maintaining white solidarity requires work. Crucially, maintaining the power and dominance of whiteness involves consistent, intricate forms of denial and dissociation that render racist realities normal, impersonal, and unremarkable. Because whiteness is inseparable from dominance, and cannot be disavowed, those of us who are white face serious perceptual limitations about the racial dimensions of reality, and our own role in perpetuating them. Those perceptual and experiential limitations are at work at the structural level, in collective behaviors and attitudes that in turn serve to maintain a status quo of racial inequality through denial and deflection. White denial operates to keep white supremacy in place at the individual and structural levels. This occurs through processes that both avoid knowledge or acknowledgement of racial benefit, and those that neutralize or naturalize that benefit, deflecting responsibility for racial ignorance and its implications. In the remainder of this chapter, I'll argue for the centrality of denial to the maintenance of white supremacy, both in individuals' attempts to navigate discrepancies between the facts and their own self-perceptions, and in political patterns that seek to locate the problem of racist violence elsewhere, outside of the liberal status quo.

WHAT IS WHITE IGNORANCE? DENIAL AS RACISM

When I teach about race, I encounter the conceptual acrobatics of white denial in my white-majority philosophy classrooms. While many are eager to learn about race and racism, every semester, a small but consistent handful of students write papers denying the current existence of racism and relegating its institutionalized manifestations to the distant past. These claims are only rarely articulated out loud, where other students can challenge them—and when they are, they are expressed as declarative outbursts. Mostly these denials are conveyed to me in essays and writing assignments, final projects and term papers that cite the critical race theorists I have assigned, while two-facedly placing medical and environmental racism, redlining, and the racialized phenomena of food deserts, gentrification, income and educational inequality, and police violence in a faraway alternate reality. If these do exist in the present, they bear no relationship to the racism that was supposedly dissolved during the civil rights era. Racism doesn't exist, and if it does, it is clearly not their problem.

My students who seek to prove that any racism that might implicate themselves ended with the civil rights era are manifesting all three kinds of denial categorized by sociologist Stanley Cohen: literal denial, interpretive denial, and implicatory denial, each of which can help us understand the seeming illogic of white cognitive resistance. Literal denials are assertions that refuse to acknowledge the facts: the facts or knowledge of them are blatantly denied, as when my students claim to have no awareness of the highly mediatized police violence experienced by non-white people.[33] This first kind of denial can be in good or bad faith, true or untrue, and can manifest as conscious or unconscious defense mechanisms.[34] A white student might be sincere in denying knowledge of racist policing, however unlikely this may seem in 2021. More likely, however, there are other forms of denial at work in addition to literal denial, like interpretive denial, which does not challenge the facts themselves, but denies their meaning. On this view, environmental racism is not really racism, but, as one of my students wrote, the result of a culture of poverty and irresponsibility in places where people of color live. Racism is intentional, directed harm committed by bad individuals, and should be condemned. But environmental racism—the disproportionate siting and impact of toxic chemical plants and waste management facilities on communities of color, compounded by lack of mobility due to redlining and other racist policies—is certainly not racism! For students who engage in interpretive denial, what has been termed environmental racism is not a phenomenon to be studied, but a phenomenon to be denied through attributions of individual blame.

This second form of denial is related to a third: implicatory denial, which does not deny the facts, but their "psychological, political, and moral implications."[35] When students claim that "racial discrimination ended in the civil rights era," the implication is that racism is a problem that need not concern them. This is a paradigm case of implicatory denial, which attempts to bridge the gap between what is acknowledged and what needs to not be known, and can also be seen in virulent opposition to critical race theory discussed in the introduction to this book. Racism may have been perpetuated by white people in the past, but, as anti-critical race theory legislation claims, this cannot have any normative implications for white people in the present. The kind of denial that denounces racism while simultaneously claiming that it either does not exist, or that it should not be "our" responsibility, attempts (unsuccessfully) to resolve the tension between what is acknowledged and what needs to not be known through evasion, avoidance, deflection, or rationalization.[36]

Each of these forms of denial can involve varying degrees of sincerity or conscious awareness. But what they all have in common is that the status of knowledge about the truth is ambiguous. This is because denial is necessarily contradictory: it is a simultaneous acceptance and disavowal of something that is "too threatening to confront, but impossible to ignore. The compromise solution is to deny and acknowledge them at the same time,"[37] to satisfy the need to "be innocent of a troubling recognition."[38] Because denial is a "perceptual defense" against disturbing emotions that might be aroused by reality,[39] it can be understood as a kind of "twilight state" between knowing and not knowing. White ignorance is precisely this kind of perceptual, moral, and political twilight state, which refuses to acknowledge, recognize, or perceive the harm and inequality of structural racism because it is difficult to reconcile with social worlds and selves made to seem normal and neutral.

The aggressiveness of denial, and the strenuous efforts made by some of my white students to neutralize and reconcile undesirable realities with their own self-perceptions and experiences of the world, indicates that there is more than obliviousness or mere indifference at work, more than a neutral absence of knowledge. We can see, rather, that white ignorance is a contradictory individual and collective state in which the impact of race and racism is simultaneously known and not known. White ignorance is a kind of denial because it selectively avoids knowledge of, and responsibility for, racism through misinterpretation, lack of acknowledgement, distancing, disavowal, dissociation, rationalization, silence, and inaction – whether or not this avoidance is self-transparent.

Understanding denial as constitutive of white ignorance—as a condition of whiteness itself—can help us make sense of its aggressive persistence in society, and not just among those who avow explicitly white supremacist views. While white ignorance is not indefeasible, as Charles Mills has written, its apparent irrationality and contradictory manifestations can be understood as entirely rational and motivated when understood as a form of protective deflection. In this sense, white ignorance is, as Jennifer C. Mueller has written, "a cognitive accomplishment grounded in explicit and tacit practices of knowing and not-knowing," characterized as much by the presence of false belief as by the "absence of understandings, feelings, and moral judgements that should be present."[40] In a world saturated with evidence of racism and "the suffering, counter-discourse, and resistance of people of color," white ignorance requires "real effort and dedication" to sustain, and those efforts are rewarded with "immense payoff."[41] This is not to equate these epistemic contortions with the political effort required to shift those collective habits and the realities they sustain, since in the first case, the effort serves to maintain white a norm of material and cognitive standing. Even if we might think of white participation in white normativity as simply "going with the flow," the effort Mueller refers to is the cognitive and emotional project of covering one's tracks when it comes to white benefit.[42] To "go with the flow" of whiteness is to simply enjoy the benefits of white cognitive standing: "more valuable and numerous material resources; feeling safe, moral, and righteous; and enjoying psychic and often literal ownership of institutional spaces."[43] What requires the effort of denial is the cognitive process that naturalizes the relationship between these benefits and whiteness, at the expense of those who are not white. These benefits in turn motivate a possessive investment in those cognitive "dysfunctions" that, because of white normativity, remain "psychologically and socially functional."[44] White ignorance is dysfunctional in its relationship to the truth about race, while being highly functional when it comes to justifying and normalizing white dominance.

Understanding white ignorance as a core process in maintaining structural racism captures the way that racial denial manifests not just in post-facto rationalizations of past racism, but as statements that guide behavior from the outset. In this way, white discourses of passivity and involuntariness in conversations about race and racism are not merely "another defense mechanism to deal with guilt, shame, or other psychic conflict after an offence has been committed"—though those post facto justifications are also a form of denial. In addition to after-the-fact justifications, white ignorance is a motivational condition "present *before* the act."[45] These "internal soliloquies" that give pre-justification to denied acts or events, or their meanings and implications, are adopted because they are politically, socially, and culturally acceptable. This is to say that a social and political system where whiteness dominates is one where denial is an embedded social, political, and institutional norm that serves the reproduction of the status quo. A status of quo maintained by white denial implies that ignorance in this case is not just a neutral lack of knowledge, not simply "faulty" or deficient cognition, but a substantive set of practices with motivations and effects.[46] While white ignorance is considered by some philosophers to be an epistemic disadvantage that limits the accuracy of white perception and understanding,[47] it is also a form of successful cognition if the goal is to protect whiteness from its own self-recognition.

SUCCESSFUL WHITE COGNITION: AGGRIEVEMENT AS A HEGEMONIC RACIAL PROJECT

White ignorance as a form of denial is a central mechanism in maintaining broader patterns of inequality. Far from being peripheral to white supremacy, or simply a symptom of it, racial avoidance that serves to keep white people "innocent of a troubling recognition" is a driver of policies that criminalize and incarcerate racialized poverty while denying the role of whiteness in the exploitation and neoliberal divestment that created it. The denial and deflection of white ignorance is key in the process of justifying racial violence and divestment as necessary for white security. As Paula Ioanide has shown, white affect is mobilized as a response to constructed racialized threats that then legitimate divestment from public goods and the expansion of the carceral state.[48] Here, I show how white ignorance—the simultaneous knowing and not-knowing by which white people avoid or fail to recognize the differential impact of race—is a crucial aspect of white racial formation and the collective pursuit of this kind of white security. A whiteness defined by primary accumulation, colonization, exploitation and racial violence deflects its own racial harm by rationalizing it as the innocent defense of an aggrieved victim.

Denial, avoidance, and deflection are certainly not new expressions and mechanisms of whiteness. But in the contemporary political and economic landscape, defined by neoliberalism and the militarized security state, whiteness is newly formulated in terms of a preservation of innocence that denies racism by positioning itself as wounded on the basis of racial identity.[49] This aggrieved whiteness "articulates a white identity of racially coded political-moral supremacy (of hard work, responsibility, and meritocratic fairness) within a worldview where this identity has been wronged by entwined forces of social liberalism and racial progress."[50] The contemporary iteration of whiteness that imagines itself to be victimized on the basis of race as it also conceives of itself as "honest, hardworking, respectable" narrates a direct reversal of a political reality that hyper-punishes the racialized poor, who have been positioned to perform the hardest forms of reproductive labor. This collective affect goes beyond simple resentment, individual bias, or even longstanding racial fear: white aggrievement is a "white identity politics aimed at maintaining white sociopolitical hegemony" and as such is the current "public face of modern white supremacy."[51] In other words, an epistemic move that not only denies, but appropriates the harm of racism in the face of evidence to the contrary, defines the current state of whiteness. Because whiteness is also associated with political, material, and social domination, we can also say that aggrieved white denial is hegemonic.

The paradigm of aggrievement finds "affective solace and self-affirmation in the punishment of the racialized poor,"[52] obfuscating histories of disenfranchisement and exploitation in order to project blame for divestment from public goods on "freeloaders." A cognitive reversal that perceives justice for racialized people as a loss to its own standing deflects attention away from oligopolies of transnational corporations, the neoliberal governments that enable them, and policies that gut support for community programs that serve the interests of racial and economic justice. Instead of recognizing neoliberal capitalism as the cause, white ignorance directs blame for social and economic problems at racialized others in the form of anti-immigrant sentiment, increased policing and incarceration of poor and working class communities of color, and defenses of white majority curricula and educational environments as a "freedom of speech" entitlement.

Such "race-making" or racializing policies and positions are not the exclusive province of right wing "extremism," but of white liberals, too, who might espouse anti-racist values while supporting political policies of sanitized divestment and "fiscal conservatism" that allow them to maintain racial innocence while enabling the punishment of the racialized poor. In fact, white ideological and political commitments have been shown to shift based on perceived demographic "status threat." That is, as a group, white people become more willing to endorse policies that will negatively impact people of color the more they perceive their own racial standing to be threatened. In other words, the need to maintain white status in order to maintain relative non-white disadvantage is an observable tendency among white people regardless of party affiliation and ideological identification.[53] Aggrievement can be more ambivalent on the left, but white leftism and white anti-racism are no strangers to it, given the hegemonic role aggrievement and denial play as the current iteration of white supremacy. As we will see in subsequent chapters, left aggrievement can manifest as an appropriation of the harm of white supremacy and racism in an effort to salvage white moral standing, and in narratives that white supremacy "hurts white people." Left white aggrievement, that claims white racial harm on account of whiteness is not analogous or equivalent to right wing narratives of losing white "ways of life." Nonetheless, the structural relationship of left-wing white aggrievement to more generalizable forms of whiteness and white dominance are important to note for white people engaged in confronting white supremacy. White supremacy is certainly damaging, and that damage is wrought through the axes of gender, class, sexual, colonial, and ableist domination. White supremacy is connected to capitalism, patriarchy, colonialism, heterosexism, and ableism. But it does not harm white people *on account of their whiteness*.

Understanding white aggrievement as a "hegemonic racial project" shows that white supremacy in its current form is not "colorblind" or oblivious to racist conditions. Rather, it has an active epistemic dimension that safeguards its structures by rationalizing their violence and reversing the narrative of racial harm. White aggrievement is not a simple passivity with respect to an unjust status quo, but a politically mobilized response to a perceived moral threat to white standing and white safety. White ignorance captures the epistemic state of that perceived moral threat, the knowledge dimension that is inseparable from white feeling and the material and political conditions of neoliberalism. In this context, "successful" white cognition functions to maintain white moral status in the face of its own efforts to also preserve its material and political status. Not all aggrievement is expressed in its right-wing form; right wing expressions are only one example of a hegemonic strategy that serves to preserve white dominance and normativity in material, social, political, emotional, and epistemic life. We can see this kind of "white panic" when white factions in left organizations decry what they perceive as the threats of "identity politics" and "cancel culture" to their own sense of political authority, rather than contending with their own participation in patterns of white domination.[54] While this left-wing expression is not synonymous with white aggrievement in its far right "vanguard" form, it is a related instance of denial and deflection as hegemonic whiteness. As many before me have shown, a commitment to anti-racism does not exempt white people from their participation in the dynamics of structural racism. As sociologist Matthew Huey has shown in his study of members of white nationalist organizations and white anti-racist groups, white "victimology" and "color capital" are key aspects of identity-formation among avowed white supremacists and anti-racists alike. It is in that sense that white aggrievement is hegemonic.[55]

A particularly insidious manifestation of hegemonic whiteness on the left is the way that neoliberal capitalism tends to reward white people for their proximity to people of color and their appropriation of non-white political struggles, so long as they do not challenge the material realities that make those struggles necessary.[56] Far from incidental, this kind of appropriation is as aspect of aggrieved whiteness in its hegemonic form. Under neoliberal capitalism, white domination is maintained by commodifying the anti-racist project in a way that deflects away from the processes that guarantee white moral, cognitive, and material advantage. Beyond being mere examples of a similar pattern, however, each manifestation plays its own role in a political ecosystem that keeps white supremacy in place.

Patterns of aggrieved white denial that operate across ideological commitments indicate that there is an epistemic dimension that links the behaviors and habits of individuals to material conditions. Frequently, "structural racism" is understood in the abstract, as a kind of invisible scaffolding that undergirds our day to day lives. While this image can be helpful for seeing beyond intentional, avowed racism as its sole manifestation, it doesn't explain how individuals mobilize their own whiteness to maintain the status quo. This is why the theory of "colorblind racism" can only take us part way in understanding how so many can support a reality that they disavow. As Mueller shows, while the theory of "colorblind racism" often used to explain structural racism does capture the way that material relations of domination organize people into races, colorblind theory neglects the connection between macrological "structures" and the local and interpersonal processes that maintain them. As a core micro and meso level mechanism by which the macrological characteristics of structural racism are maintained, ignorance is the missing piece. Without an account of the denial and evasions of white ignorance, we cannot understand what the elements of "colorblind" racism—abstract liberalism, naturalization, cultural racism, and minimization—look like in practice.[57]

More accurate than the ableist term "colorblind," which implies that white racism on the part of individuals is unwitting or mere cognitive limitation and that structural racism is an abstraction operating beyond the rational intentions of individuals, the language of ignorance and denial can help explain the collective stakes and motivations that uphold racist institutions, policies, and norms. White ignorance—whether conscious or unconscious—is a way of maintaining the benefits of race-based domination without appearing "deviant" or "immoral" to oneself or others. In this way, systems that give some undeserved racial advantage over others can be maintained, precisely because those who benefit from them can disavow that benefit and its basis. Mueller has called this pattern of disavowal "successful white cognition," since it allows knowers with a broad range of ideological commitments to abide by racist norms without the moral taint of "being racist."[58]

Beyond "obliviousness" about race and racism, this kind of successful white cognition is hyper-aware of the moral threat of being judged as racist, and actively defensive about this accusation even before the charge is made. In the same way that, as we saw with Cohen, denial is not post-facto but part of the background conditions, successful white cognition is "in" aggrieved denial even before material, cognitive, and moral benefit are deliberately pursued. This pattern of default white self-protection against the threat of losing illicit moral and cognitive status is a structural phenomenon that operates across class and identity. It is hegemonic because it shows up in liberal and left discourse as well as in right wing discourses of white aggrievement. Indeed, as Cohen shows, most white people living under conditions of apartheid, genocide, or racial injustice seek to resolve troubling or upsetting contradictions between their sense of self and their circumstances through neutralizations, rationalizations, avoidances, and deflections. In this way, white ignorance projects the unpleasantness, discomfort, and distress that accompanies the awareness of racial harm and/or a loss of cognitive and moral status on racialized others, while attributing the explicit desire to maintain white dominance to white poor and working class people alone—another deflection that maintains white supremacy by always attributing responsibility to someone else.

LIBERALISM AND THE DISPLACEMENT OF RACISM

White deflection is also a political pattern that limits the forms of political participation we think are possible. The political corollary to "successful white speech" is the way that liberal democracies like the US, Canada, France, and the UK position themselves as racially neutral relative to the far right, while maintaining a racist status quo that hyperexploits and contains migrants and people of color through militarized policing, hyperincerceration, and organized abandonment. As Aaron Winter and Aurelien Mondon write in *Reactionary Democracy*, the perception that far right groups are "white supremacist" while liberal whites are racially innocent is an old, and incorrect trope that maintains the normativity of whiteness, positioning the status quo as the only alternative to illiberal, anti-democratic forms of whiteness like white nationalism and other far-right movements.[59] This viewpoint is a form of displacement, distancing itself from the more extreme iterations of racism espoused by those considered far right radicals. However, as Mondon and Winter write, "illiberal racism (and with it both the extreme right and far right) is not an autonomous, ahistorical form, but a contingent and functional one that allows liberal societies to represent themselves as post-racist."[60] Far right ideology arises out of material conditions maintained by liberalism. The far right, constructed as "extreme" relative to the status quo, occupies a position such that the political mainstream can claim racial innocence and neutrality, and even injury, when it is made to face its own basis in white supremacy.

A well-documented example of this injured deflection is the so-called debate about "freedom of speech," a weaponization and appropriation of the left-wing language of the 1960s and undefined liberal abstractions to agitate for reactionary and discredited ideas, while claiming that this stance is being censored by the "woke" social justice establishment.[61] This current liberal paradigm, which makes space for virulent, racist, sexist, and homophobic ideas under the auspices of "free" debate, maintains a political dynamic where systemic material injustices cannot be addressed and are reduced to "mere offensiveness with nothing at stake for those targeted."[62] The reversal is striking: the mostly white and mostly male defenders of the reactionary "free speech" paradigm claim that their injury when prevented from debating the reality of racism, sexism, or the Holocaust is based in enlightenment rationality and universalism, while those whose life chances were impacted by these events are too-sensitive, coddled "snowflakes."

It might not be immediately evident what claims to "free speech" and "free debate" have to do with whiteness and the epistemic defenses of its dominance. But it does not take a very close inspection to see that the primary function of the "free speech" movement is the literal repression of knowledge-production about race and racism. This movement is organized and funded beyond Trump's now defunct 1776 Project, and is particularly active in educational policy, as we have seen with the critical race theory "debates." In some instances, parents have pulled their children out of school, claiming that "wokeness" and "social justice curricula" are limiting their child's right to a "free" education, and their own right to "free speech." In this sense, the free speech movement is a paradigm case of hegemonic white aggrievement that takes the acknowledgement of racism as a violation of white standing. While the concept of freedom of speech is rarely defined by proponents of free speech as the legally codified right that it is, it is taken up not only to deny the existence of racism, but claim that white people like its proponents are its truest victims. Jordan Peterson, for example, has notoriously claimed that an accusation of racism directed at him is "racist in its extreme."[63] Proponents of "free speech" tend to make the facile claim that exposing white people to histories of racism is a violation of their rights—a view held widely by liberals, conservatives, and those on the far and mainstream right that understands racial justice and the knowledges associated with it as "injustices" to white people.

These forms of militant liberal denial and reversal are not extreme, but dominant. The well-documented outcome of this dynamic has been to categorize the anti-racist left as a form of anti-liberal "extremism" analogous to the far right, while white nationalism is normalized and legitimated—as we saw with the differential treatment of Black Lives Matter protesters and those who stormed the US Capitol. To view "extremism" as the cause of white terror diverts attention away from the mainstream normativity of white violence, and its role in creating fertile ground for far right movements. It positions Black and anti-capitalist resistance in particular as an extremist threat to be suppressed, as we have seen with US counter-intelligence initiatives, and the surveilling and detaining of Black and anti-capitalist activists. This is why scholars like Dan Berger and Joy James have argued that mass incarceration is a means for politically repressing people of color resistance and movements for racial justice.[64]

To disavow the interconnections between liberal racism and far right racism also incorrectly assumes that far right discourse does not understand itself as race-neutral, or engage in racial deflection. Far right groups, as Matthew Lyons has shown, represent a range of ideological positions, with many claiming (contradictorily) to espouse race-neutrality rather than white supremacy. The Proud Boys and the Oath Keepers, for example, see themselves as "Western chauvinist" rather than white supremacist or even white nationalist, each group touting its (very few) non-white members as examples of race-neutrality, even while defending oppressive policies that have direct racist impact. The same can be said of some white nationalist groups, or even of "Alt Right" groups who claim, sometimes in earnest, to be in favor of "race neutral" individualist libertarianism, all the while embracing explicitly anti-Semitic tropes and coded discourses of white superiority. Many far right groups—and many who showed up at the Capitol on January 6, 2021—are anti-capitalist or anti-imperialist.[65] To be clear: these groups are at the vanguard of white supremacist ideology. But what is most relevant about their inconsistencies is the denial of racism at their core, which scholars like Lyons understand to be *the* contemporary mode of racist discourse, rather than its concealment. Denial of racism, in other words, is synonymous with racism. And the shape of this denial can be seen anywhere where people are white.

CONCLUSION

In this chapter, I have argued that racial ignorance and denial are central to whiteness and the maintenance of white supremacy. This includes denial of white supremacy itself; to deny whiteness and its role simply is *the* contemporary character of racism, with manifestations that range from anti-racist appropriations of racial grievance to the mass incarceration of Black and brown people. I showed that white ignorance is not merely psychological, cultural, or even epistemic in the traditional sense, but a structural and political phenomenon that has to do with maintaining the benefit and access associated with whiteness without having to appear racist (and thus lose moral standing). The emotions of individual white people certainly play a role in maintaining domination. But we cannot capture the contradictory and seemingly nonsensical nature of the behaviors of white people without grasping their structural context, and situating them within a hegemonic "twilight state" that manages the moral threat of acknowledging participation in systems of racial benefit. It is in this sense that white ignorance is the epistemic dimension of white supremacy.

White ignorance as a form of hegemonic racial denial is significant not only in its being widespread beyond the far right, but in the deflective role that it occupies in the political landscape. Literal, interpretive, and implicatory denial are central to the way that abstract liberalist discourse like freedom of speech, the naturalization of racial injustice, cultural racism, and the minimization of the role of race operate. We cannot understand the perpetuation of these "colorblind" macro-patterns without the role of racial ignorance as a micro and meso process. Because white ignorance is a form of denial that has the character of a "twilight state" of simultaneous knowing and not-knowing that serves to keep white people "innocent of a troubling recognition," it can help explain the aggrievement and resistance expressed by white people across the political spectrum, who see themselves as having something to lose on the basis of race, while denying the reality of undeserved racial benefit. It can also help us explain political discourses that deflect mainstream racism by using events like the January 6th attack on the Capitol as a repository for racial blame, while the conditions that give rise to everyday racial violence persist.

Reversals, obfuscations, displacements and disassociations that justify, obscure, and maintain racial violence and suppression for white benefit are the very building blocks of whiteness. This means that knowledge acquisition will only get us so far, since denial and ignorance are not simply a passive absence of information, but broad range of substantive practices and patterns tied to maintaining realities of racial inequality. As my students' papers show, facts will be resisted by white denial if we don't simultaneously address other registers of white supremacy like habit formation, emotional and affective response, and access to land and the material means to flourish for non-white people. Knowledge and ignorance cannot be understood outside of entrenched systems of colonial and racist benefit and exploitation. White ignorance is structural insofar as it denies the role of race in the social order, shifting the blame onto "others," when it is in fact a pervasive force embedded in our laws and norms, and reproduced through white suppression of challenges to white standing. The upshot is facing the paradoxical task of challenging whiteness' claim to innocence in the face of threats to its own moral status.

NOTES

1. Anand Giridharadas, "The January 6 Insurrection Was a Last Gasp for White Supremacy," accessed May 11, 2021, https://www.msnbc.com/the-last-word/watch/the-january-6-insurrection-was-a-last-gasp-for-white-supremacy-99557445706.

2. Dwight R. Boyd, *Becoming of Two Minds about Liberalism: A Chronicle of Philosophical and Moral Development* (Springer, 2015), 240; Barbara Applebaum, *Being White, Being Good: White Complicity, White Moral Responsibility, and Social Justice Pedagogy* (Lexington Books, 2010), 53.

3. Charles W. Mills, "White Ignorance," in *Race and Epistemologies of Ignorance*, ed. Nancy Tuana and Shannon Sullivan (Albany: SUNY Press, 2012), 20.

4. Mills, 13.

5. Miranda Fricker, *Epistemic Injustice: Power and the Ethics of Knowing* (Clarendon Press, 2007). Fricker has called this phenomenon "testimonial injustice": where a speaker receives unfair credibility as a result of their membership in a socially or culturally dominant group.

6. Charles Wade Mills, *Black Rights/White Wrongs: The Critique of Racial Liberalism* (Oxford University Press, 2017).

7. Ruth Wilson Gilmore, *Golden Gulag: Prisons, Surplus, Crisis, and Opposition in Globalizing California* (University of California Press, 2007), 28.

8. Iris Marion Young, "The Five Faces of Oppression," *The Philosophical Forum* XIX, no. 4 (1988): 270–90.

9. Noel Ignatiev, *How the Irish Became White* (Routledge, 2012); Karen Brodkin, *How Jews Became White Folks and What That Says about Race in America* (Rutgers University Press, 1998); Ian Haney Lopez, *White by Law: The Legal Construction of Race* (NYU Press, 1996).

10. Linda Martín Alcoff, *The Future of Whiteness* (John Wiley & Sons, 2015).

11. Paula Ioanide, "Defensive Appropriations," in *Antiracism Inc. : Why the Way We Talk about Racial Justice Matters*, ed. Felice Blake, Alison Reed, and Paula Ioanide (Brooklyn, NY: punctum books, 2019), 83–107; Cheryl I. Harris, "Whiteness as Property," *Harvard Law Review* 106, no. 8 (1993): 1707–91.

12. Kenneth Jones and Tema Okun, *Dismantling Racism: A Workbook for Social Change Groups* (Changework, 2001), https://resourcegeneration.org/wp-content/uploads/2018/01/2016-dRworks-workbook.pdf.

13. Baldwin, James, "On Being 'White' . . . And Other Lies," in *Black On White: Black Writers on What It Means to Be White* (New York: Schocken Books, 1998).

14. George Yancy, *Look, A White!: Philosophical Essays on Whiteness* (Temple University Press, 2012), 166.

15. Robyn Wiegman, *Object Lessons* (Duke University Press, 2012), 186.

16. Robin DiAngelo and Michael Eric Dyson, *White Fragility: Why It's So Hard for White People to Talk about Racism*, reprint edition (Boston: Beacon Press, 2018).

17. W. E. B. Du Bois, *Black Reconstruction in America: Toward a History of the Part Which Black Folk Played in the Attempt to Reconstruct Democracy in America, 1860–1880* (Transaction Publishers, 2013); Chris Crass, Chris Dixon, and Roxanne Dunbar-Ortiz, *Towards Collective Liberation: Anti-Racist Organizing, Feminist Praxis, and Movement Building Strategy*, 2013; David R. Roediger and Kendrick C. Babcock Professor of History David R. Roediger, *The Wages of Whiteness: Race and the Making of the American Working Class* (Verso, 1999).

18. Du Bois, *Black Reconstruction in America.*

19. Joel Olson, *The Abolition of White Democracy* (University of Minnesota Press, 2004), 3.

20. Olson.

21. Cedric J. Robinson, *Black Marxism: The Making of the Black Radical Tradition* (University of North Carolina Press, 2005).

22. Christina Zhao, "Coca-Cola, Facing Backlash, Says 'Be Less White' Learning Plan Was About Workplace Inclusion," *Newsweek*, February 21, 2021, https://www.newsweek.com/coca-cola-facing-backlash-says-less-white-learning-plan-was-about-workplace-inclusion-1570875.

23. Robinson, *Black Marxism.*

24. Gerald Horne, *The Dawning of the Apocalypse: The Roots of Slavery, White Supremacy, Settler Colonialism, and Capitalism in the Long Sixteenth Century* (NYU Press, 2020).

25. Walter Rodney, *How Europe Underdeveloped Africa* (Verso Books, 2018); Horne, *The Dawning of the Apocalypse*.

26. Du Bois, *Black Reconstruction in America.*

27. J. Sakai, *Settlers: The Mythology of the White Proletariat from Mayflower to Modern* (PM Press, 2014).

28. Lateiner, in Heather McGhee, *The Sum of Us: What Racism Costs Everyone and How We Can Prosper Together* (Random House Publishing Group, 2021), 240.

29. Jordan T. Camp, *Incarcerating the Crisis: Freedom Struggles and the Rise of the Neoliberal State* (University of California Press, 2016).

30. McGhee, *The Sum of Us*.

31. Yancy, *Look, A White!*, 165.

32. Nikhil Pal Singh, "A Note on Race and the Left," *Social Text*, accessed July 13, 2021, https://socialtextjournal.org/a-note-on-race-and-the-left/.

33. Stanley Cohen, *States of Denial: Knowing about Atrocities and Suffering* (John Wiley & Sons, 2013), 7.

34. Ibid.

35. Ibid., 8.

36. Ibid.

37. Ibid., 27.

38. Ibid., 25.

39. Ibid., 4.

40. Jennifer C. Mueller, "Racial Ideology or Racial Ignorance? An Alternative Theory of Racial Cognition," *Sociological Theory* 38, no. 2 (June 2020): 142–69, 146.

41. Ibid., 147.

42. Crass, Dixon, and Dunbar-Ortiz, *Towards Collective Liberation.*

43. Mueller, "Racial Ideology or Racial Ignorance?", 147.

44. George Lipsitz, *The Possessive Investment in Whiteness: How White People Profit from Identity Politics* (Temple University Press, 2018).

45. Cohen, *States of Denial,* 58.

46. Linda Martín Alcoff, "Epistemologies of Ignorance: Three Types," in *Race and Epistemologies of Ignorance*, ed. Nancy Tuana and Shannon Sullivan (Albany: SUNY Press, 2012), 39–57, 40.

47. José Medina, *The Epistemology of Resistance: Gender and Racial Oppression, Epistemic Injustice, and Resistant Imaginations,* (Oxford : Oxford University Press, 2012).

48. Paula Ioanide, *The Emotional Politics of Racism: How Feelings Trump Facts in an Era of Colorblindness* (Stanford University Press, 2015).

49. Mike King, "Aggrieved Whiteness: White Identity Politics and Modern American Racial Formation," in *Making Abolitionist Worlds*, Abolition Collective (Philadelphia: Common Notions, 2020).

50. King, 143.

51. Ibid., 134–135.

52. Ibid., 140.

53. Maureen A. Craig and Jennifer A. Richeson, "On the Precipice of a 'Majority-Minority' America: Perceived Status Threat from the Racial Demographic Shift Affects White Americans' Political Ideology," *Psychological Science* 25, no. 6 (June 1, 2014): 1189–97, https://doi.org/10.1177/0956797614527113.

54. Henry Giroux, in Chip Berlet, *Eyes Right!: Challenging the Right Wing Backlash* (South End Press, 1995).

55. Matthew Hughey, *White Bound: Nationalists, Antiracists, and the Shared Meanings of Race* (Stanford University Press, 2012).

56. Marlon Peterson, in Akiba Solomon and Kenrya Rankin, *How We Fight White Supremacy: A Field Guide to Black Resistance* (PublicAffairs, 2019).

57. Eduardo Bonilla-Silva, *Racism without Racists: Color-Blind Racism and the Persistence of Racial Inequality in the United States* (Rowman & Littlefield Publishers, 2006).

58. Mueller, "Racial Ideology or Racial Ignorance?", 156.

59. Aurelien Mondon and Aaron Winter, *Reactionary Democracy: How Racism and the Populist Far Right Became Mainstream*, 2020.

60. Mondon and Winter, 49.

61. Ibid., 80.

62. Ibid., 70.

63. Ibid., 86.

64. Dan Berger, *The Struggle Within: Prisons, Political Prisoners, and Mass Movements in the United States* (PM Press, 2014); Joy James, *The New Abolitionists: (Neo)Slave Narratives and Contemporary Prison Writings* (SUNY Press, 2005).

65. Matthew N. Lyons, *Insurgent Supremacists: The U.S. Far Right's Challenge to State and Empire* (PM Press, 2018).

Chapter 2

Declarations and Absolutions

Moral Paradoxes of White Ignorance

In the summer of 2020 the two block radius around my apartment was the site of a major uprising. In the weeks and months after George Floyd was murdered, Black Lives Matter marches went past my window; police set up military-style staging areas around the corner near the bus stop; and when chain stores were looted and a building went up in flames one block over, I watched armored SWAT team tanks roll past my house, shooting rubber bullets and tear gas. After a particularly tense night, I woke up with my throat and eyes burning from the tear gas that had saturated the air inside my apartment. Only months later, again a few blocks away, Walter Wallace Jr. was shot and killed by police when his mother called for support in getting him through a mental health episode. This was in West Philadelphia, the historically Black neighborhood where city police terrorized, bombed, and burned down the house of the MOVE family in the 1980s. While the violent police occupation of my block was terrifying and viscerally affecting, I knew that it was not meant primarily for me, a white gentrifier. But the racial dynamics of those particular protests and confrontations did prompt some difficult questions about white agency that defied any trite or generalizable definitions of "allyship," "accompliceship," or "following Black leadership."

One memorable evening brought the paradox of white anti-racism into sharp relief. After the murder of Walter Wallace Jr., the local chapter of Black Lives Matter and the MOVE Organization called for a march through West Philadelphia to the police precinct near the site of the murder. The march was Black-led, but white-majority. As we marched through Cobbs Creek—a neighborhood that is 93% Black—some residents cheered from their porches, but many looked on with skepticism or even derision. One woman admonished us for our lackluster chanting, and began leading the chanting herself from in front of her house. A few blocks later, a man standing on the sidewalk shouted, rhetorically, "What are you doing here?" As an organizer began to speak with the man, the march came to a halt on a residential street. We stood there, a group of mostly white protesters, with an audience of mostly Black people, in what I remember as an uneasy quiet. The answer that we were there to show that we cared for Black lives deflated even before it could be uttered aloud. Cobbs Creek is a neighborhood where the presence of white people has historically meant violence or displacement. What were we doing there indeed?

Rather than offer a corrective way to engage in protest or give a retrospective answer to the "what should white people do" question with respect to the 2020 uprisings, this chapter surveys the difficult moral terrain of white anti-racism to identify some of its contradictions and their moral origins. Chapter 1 defined white ignorance as a form of denial and deflection—a need not to know. This chapter describes the ways that white ignorance can manifest even in white attempts to overcome it through racial knowledge. White ignorance is an actively managed, substantive form of avoidance, and not just a neutral absence of information. For this reason, claiming knowledge of racism, or declaring one's lack of knowledge, can each serve as their own kind of evasion. Whether one seeks to demonstrate one's desire to be anti-racist or performatively declares one's need to learn, white-anti racism participates in a moral economy centered on white moral absolution. Thus, white responses to racism exist in a paradoxical space of simultaneous performance and sincerity, accountability and failure. The "twilight state" of white ignorance is not just epistemological, but moral, too.

In this chapter, I describe the ways that white moral and political responses to racism, while necessary, are plagued by the risk of reproducing undeserved white moral capital and authority. I begin by situating moralities of white redemption in the context of Protestant justifications of colonial expropriation and white "mastery" over enslaved people. I trace the lineage of white saviorism back to strains of early US Protestantism that linked spiritual responsibility and whiteness. This origin story helps explain some of the specific ways that race continues to be the terrain for establishing white moral standing in settler societies like the US. The remainder of the chapter finds the white Protestant themes of moral absolution and spiritual access in two case studies: "white talk" in the classroom, and institutional declarations of anti-racism. I show that in each case, we can see the traces of white Protestant morality in responses to racial harm that center white agency in the project of maintaining white innocence. In the case of "white talk," a deflective "fluttering" around race that aims to signal white moral standing, the settler Protestant desire to be one of the moral and spiritual "elect" shows up in white students' entitlement to the presence and experiences of students of color. I draw on sociological research on students in multi-racial classrooms to show that white ignorance manifests in white projects to secure moral rectitude with respect to race. Race, and the dynamics of racial difference and colonial appropriation, continue to be the terrain on which white ideologies of mastery and moral authority are reproduced. The second example of white settler morality I feature in this chapter are institutional declarations of racism or anti-racism, that, like the example of white talk, instrumentalize race and racism in order to inoculate against the charge of moral and political taint. Like white talk, declarative admissions and confessions of racial guilt also function to secure both moral and material standing. In each case, performances of racial guilt, apology, and the desire to know and learn are used protectively and deflectively. These declarations and absolutions work to maintain social and institutional environments that reward white people materially, psychically, and spiritually, reproducing old colonial dynamics that serve the interests of white capital under the auspices of benevolent white goodness.

For white people dismayed about their participation in racial harm, there is no easy way around what Claudia Rankine has called "the reparative largesse of whiteness in the face of human pain and suffering,"[1] or what others have called the "white savior complex." These tendencies reproduce white superiority and moral satisfaction while claiming to do the opposite, all the while obscuring the role of non-white resistance. We saw in chapter 1 that white ignorance is an actively managed, hegemonic "twilight state" between knowing and not knowing. The examples in this chapter—white talk and institutional declarations of guilt or innocence—shine a spotlight on the moral dimension of white ignorance, the origins of which can be traced back to moral justifications for the colonial mastery over and seizure of land, bodies, and labor. We can see in each of these examples the reverberations of moralities that instrumentalize race and racial difference for the purposes of an individual salvation inseparable from the rationalization of material domination. This reveals a problem: white supremacy has warped our notions of responsibility and accountability, and is at work in the very moral frameworks we use to address it. When these moral frameworks are based in binary moralities of sin and salvation, guilt and innocence, taint and purity, they run a high risk of reproducing the conditions of racial harm. Making responsibility and accountability synonymous with individual absolution and redemption—as many mainstream moral frameworks do—draws resources, attention, and self-determination away from those most affected by racial harm. Rather than reject the project of white accountability, however (as current conservative and far-right groups are so eager to do), this chapter troubles notions of moral responsibility predicated on individual absolution in order to make way for a different approach.

SITUATING WHITE MORAL CAPITAL: SETTLER MORALITIES OF MASTERY

The "reparative largesse of whiteness" that positions white people as the central moral agents in the face of racial harm has deep historical roots. As decolonial feminists have shown so clearly, the white savior is not a *sui generis* phenomenon, but is produced through material conditions of colonial domination, reinforcing the notion that colonized populations are "primitive" and in need of "civilizing" by benevolent colonizers.[2] This colonial paradigm of responsibility links responsible agency to the establishment of innocence insofar as benevolent acts undertaken by white colonizers save colonized people from their own supposed inferiority, while also saving the souls of the colonizers through "good works" that relieve the moral pressure caused by the violence of occupation.[3] We can recognize this colonial paradigm rooted in Christian morality in demonstrative white "helping" in the US: If we understand the US as a settler colony in the present tense, the risk of colonial-style "white saviorism" in contemporary racial justice movements isn't merely metaphorical, but literal. For this reason, looking at the colonial origins of discourses of individual redemption, and their material motivations, can help us understand a contemporary moral landscape that includes theocratic white nationalism on the far right, the complex legacy of abolitionism on the left, and an establishment and non-profit industrial complex in between. The tangled strands of this history have origins in colonial Puritan and Protestant moral philosophies characterized by an ethos of individual salvation and spiritual status through "settlement" (land theft) and work—and are inherently raced.

Philip L. Berg writes in "Racism and the Puritan Mind" that beyond the "peculiar machinations of modern American capitalism and democracy," the moral ideologies of early Protestant settlers can help us understand the "inconsistencies" of contemporary racism, namely the way that white people deny racial prejudice while blaming inequality on the deficient behavior of non-white people.[4] To understand this "ambivalence in racial attitudes" we must look to colonial Puritanism, which understood the "Errand Into The Wilderness as . . .a holy experiment" meant to demonstrate that "God rewards those who live by his word."[5] Puritan doctrines of divine election that accord moral and spiritual agency to white settlers are, according to Berg, very much alive today,

> as can be seen by the manner in which many white Americans conceive of the race problem. Like their Puritan forebears, white Americans today are disinclined to examine the nature of the American social structure itself in their search for an explanation of racial problems. They are far more likely to adopt

> the Puritan posture of casting a baleful stare at those who do not appear to be living up to the exalted purposes of the Grand American Design, and condemning them for their willful lack of commitment to it. The Puritan mentality, then, is still with us: only the "vocabulary of motives" has changed.[6]

Berg's "Puritan mentality" is only one of a cluster of white Protestant moralities that emerged during crucial moments of colonial consolidation, particularly in interaction with questions of slavery and freedom. The colonial project in the so-called New World did coincide with the advent of political liberalism, which, while it claimed secularism, was informed by Immanuel Kant's pietism and its heavenly "Kingdom of Ends" populated only with those capable of rational free will; John Locke's justification of property based on God's will and conception of humans as God's property; and Hugo Grotius's uptake of the Aristotelian notion that some are natural slaves. Many theorists have already done the work of exposing the racism built into social contract theory and the assumed whiteness of the modern, liberal subject.[7] What I am suggesting here is that the ground for these European philosophies was prepared not just by Christianity writ large, but by the interplay of Protestant doctrine with colonial imperatives to claim entitlement to land and non-white bodies as its own form of religious salvation. Looking at the on-the-ground development of settlement linked to both religion and race can help us understand white imperatives to be racially "good" in the neoliberal era as rooted in long-standing moral economies of white mastery. As historian Katharine Gerbner writes of the racing of morality among seventeenth century settlers, "Protestant slave owners would use religion to define mastery and police their enslaved population. They developed an ideology of Protestant Supremacy that linked Christian status to mastery and whiteness."[8] While this exclusive claim to spiritual legitimacy was initially challenged by missionaries, imperial officials, and enslaved and free people of African descent, Christian debates about the status of one's soul and access to salvation were motivated by the need to justify racial exploitation and dominance.

Rather than downplaying the role of Protestant Christianity in the settlement of the US by understanding planter and settler life as "depraved," as many historians have (including Du Bois in *Black Reconstruction in America*), it's helpful to see Protestantism and Protestant Supremacy as the causal predecessors of the ideology of white supremacy that emerged as racial slavery was codified.[9] Far from being analytically separable from white supremacy, US Protestantism developed ideas of spiritual mastery in direct relation to the status of "master" in relation to "slave." While other forms of Christianity like Anglicanism and Catholicism were involved in colonial projects, what set the US apart was the reluctance of the Protestant settler majority to allow non-white conversion out of a concern to reserve "elect" status for white people—that is, religious entitlement to land and the ownership of enslaved people as divinely ordained. While initially, settler Protestantism (especially the iterations adopted by the planter class) could not countenance the conversion of non-white people, since religion was what differentiated slavery and freedom, a new US formulation that Gerbner calls "Christian Slavery" was soon brought onto the scene in order to render slavery compatible with Protestantism—that is, to make it possible to be both a Christian and a slave. The idea of Christian Slavery drew on "biblical descriptions of slavery as well as the ideal of the godly household to encourage slave owners to assume responsibility for the spiritual lives of their enslaved laborers," eventually emphasizing "the beneficial aspects of slave conversion" in terms of docility and productivity[10]—the same justifications employed into the 19th and 20th centuries in residential schools that aimed to "kill the Indian to save the man."

The development of Afro-Protestantism even before the eighteenth century might seem to challenge the relationship between the Protestant ethos and white racial mastery. But, as Gerbner documents, planters' desire to prevent enslaved people from accessing Christian knowledge in the seventeenth and eighteenth centuries by prohibiting access to literacy, books, and Christian ritual "made Christianity a sign of mastery and power."[11] As significant numbers of Africans and Afro-Caribbeans eventually gained access to Christian rites like baptism, slave owners adapted by replacing "Christian" with "white" as an indicator of freedom and mastery.[12] From the beginning of colonial nation-formation, who was entitled to salvation was linked to power and racial domination.

The pattern of maintaining white protection from sin through exclusive access to the tools of salvation, while leaving the material conditions of racial domination unchallenged, persisted into the nineteenth and twentieth centuries. Even early white anti-slavery, especially among Quakers, argued against the practice on the grounds that it was a moral taint on the souls of white people.[13] This kind of argument supported nineteenth century "colonization" schemes that proposed to solve the moral problem of slavery by removing people of African descent from the continental US, or the forms of "gradualism" advocated by early white abolitionists that sought to end the slave trade without ending the practice of slavery itself. To be sure, this does not represent abolitionist movements as whole, particularly if we center Black abolitionists in the history of the movement. These examples serve, rather, to show how a white Protestant paradigm positioned those who benefitted from racial exploitation as those entitled to solve the problem of their own racial harm, with their own moral status in mind.

The moral economies that are the backdrop for contemporary white responses to racism in settler colonies can be traced back to the ways that Protestant moralities connected colonization and enslavement. By looking at the moral discourses that emerged along with the taking of land and bodies, we can begin to outline a spiritual territoriality that responded defensively to the ways that Black and non-white conversion and subversion changed Christian practice. This shows that white ignorance is tenacious because it protects the moral and material capital extracted through political domination. These histories of mastery show that the Protestant work ethic is not only capitalist, but racist, too. Identified by sociologist Max Weber, the Protestant work ethic refers to the capitalist transmutation of Calvinist private salvation into self-disciplined, profitable work. In keeping with Puritan colonial morality, the US white Protestant ethos holds that "only an elect few are predestined for salvation from birth, while the rest are damned."[14] As Alana Massey writes, "the anxiety that this produced compelled people to look for hints or signs that they were members of the elect; they believed that material success was among the most notable indicators of God's favor."[15] This is to say that there is a moral economy of white supremacy bound up with its political economy. Those who have benefitted from colonial expropriation and accumulation are justified as its moral protagonists and responsible agents in the drama of racial harm. This moral paradigm positions white people at center stage, dependent on non-white presence to resolve the tensions in the story, while denying that it has written the script. In this way, white people who wish to take responsibility for white supremacy find themselves in a moral economy set up to preserve their own innocence and moral capital. This set of moral relations positions them to perpetuate racial harm even in their efforts to absolve themselves of it.

MORAL RELIEF IN KNOWLEDGE: WHITE TALK AND THE ENTITLEMENT TO KNOW

One does not have to identify as Protestant or subscribe in a self-aware way to the colonial entitlement to land to embody settler moralities rooted in Protestantism. Because whiteness was constructed by the possibility of property ownership and belonging within a raced and religiously delineated political and moral community, it would be strange if that position did not manifest in moral behavior. As we saw in chapter 1, the need to protect innocence from the troubling recognition of one's own participation in racial harm is constitutive of whiteness; white moral behavior and white material benefit are co-constituting. This section looks at racial-virtue-signaling speech patterns—"white talk"—as a mode of establishing white moral status, even and especially when it signals racial knowledge. It is of course wrongheaded to say that learning about racism is wrong. More than a desire to learn, however, white talk performs that desire, or uses knowledge about racism, as a badge of moral protection from the moral taint of being racist. If one shows that one knows—that one has this special knowledge, or seeks to access it—one establishes oneself as a "good white person." White talk is an example of settler morality because it uses non-white and colonized people, and the dynamics of racial and colonial difference, to enact rituals of white salvation.

"White talk" describes patterns of speech that signal racial goodness. Expressions of white talk include performative outrage at racism, hints that one isn't one of *those* white people, indications of one's anti-racist activities, coded language that seeks to demonstrate knowledge of people of color—and resentment when opportunities for these expressions are denied, or when they are not well-received by non-white people. "White talk," even if it sometimes talks directly about race, is a culturally sanctioned evasion discourse that functions to "insulate White people from examining their/our individual and collective role(s) in the perpetuation of racism," and that "protects the interests of the privileged and their moral composure."[16] Alison Bailey has described white talk as "fluttering" around the fear of finding oneself complicit in structural racism, an evasiveness "designed, indeed scripted, for the purposes of evading, rejecting, and remaining ignorant about the injustices that flow from whiteness and its attendant privileges."[17] White talk persists, Bailey writes, because "it has powerful moral, ontological and epistemic payoff for white folks" in construing them as morally "invulnerable."[18] It serves to construct the speaker as an imagined, well-meaning, non-racist white self to whom white people "can boomerang back when we feel that our perceived sense of ourselves as not racist is being challenged."[19] Bailey writes that this kind of discourse acts as a "ritual of moral purification that seeks to evoke people of color's affirmation" that the speaker is not racist. Similar to past expressions of white settler moral economies, white talk enlists non-white people in the drama of its own salvation.

It's easy to condemn white talk as mere "bad behavior," but white talk is often *both* sincerely well-meaning, and also a performance of well-meaningness meant to convey one's anti-racism. It is a speech pattern embedded in material conditions that distribute both moral and material capital unequally. Whether or not it is self-aware, and irrespective of its intended impact, white talk centers white moral rectitude, occluding the recognition of the grievances of non-white people in the service of whites' *identity* as morally good white people. As Rachel McKinnon has written, those who identity as "allies" tend to overestimate their effectiveness in anti-racist efforts,[20] and tend to react negatively to constructive criticism. What is behind this resistance is a desire not only to not be bad, but for moral standing relative to other whites accorded through the real or imagined labor of people of color. In other words, the desire to be a good white doesn't just involve the denial of complicity; it also exploits real and imagined people of color as arbiters in a moral contest that centers, features, and is directed by, whites.[21] Such everyday performances of anti-racism, then, run the risk of reproducing white dominance both morally and epistemically.

White talk is a well-documented phenomenon, and social justice educators have given serious attention to the persistence of its discursive patterns in the classroom. It was found in a study by Kim Case and Annette Hennings, for example, that the majority of white pre-service women teachers responded to questions about racism in such a way as to avoid being viewed as racist or as implicated in systemic oppression.[22] Kathy Hytten and John Warren catalogue these "tactics" in their own ethnographies, listing these forms of avoidance as "remaining silent, evading questions, resorting to the rhetoric of ignoring color, focusing on progress, victim blaming and focusing on culture rather than race."[23] Hytten and Warren note that these discursive moves are "culturally sanctioned"; they are "already available, already common forms of asserting dominance" by claiming rightness and denying the racism of their own habits.[24] As Barbara Applebaum writes, "white ignorance is not only sustained by denials of complicity but white ignorance also authorizes such denials," actively resisting any input that challenges innocence by appealing to normative or dominant explanations and concepts.[25] This discursive resistance can manifest as simple "disagreement" with the course material, though these denials are socially authorized ways of "protecting the center, the location of privilege" (Ibid.). McIntyre calls this "privileged choice"; Peggy McIntosh, author of the much cited "White Privilege: Unpacking the Invisible Knapsack," calls it "permission to escape," because students' ability to dismiss systemic oppression as an opinion with which they can disagree is a function of the privilege of choice to disengage from discussions of systemic oppression. What these students' discursive tactics betray is a deep investment in moral innocence which the subjects fear will become destabilized if they engage critically with questions of race.

Scholarship on white talk tends to focus on it as avoidance or distancing as such. I argue, however, that this denial is substantive, linked to moral economies that position white people as moral agents rather than passive avoiders. As we saw in chapter 1, denial is inherently contradictory, seeking to preserve innocence precisely because on some level—even if not fully conscious—there is some recognition of participating in harm; otherwise there would be nothing to avoid. In this vein, Bailey includes statements like, "I'm a lesbian, so I understand oppression" in her list of examples of white talk, a statement meant to indicate racial knowledge, to show that one knows. These kinds of demonstrative statements are not literal denials, but are forms of implicatory denial, that use knowledge to preemptively deflect blame and establish racial innocence. In this peculiar manifestation of white ignorance, knowledge acquisition is experienced as a purifying ritual or talisman to ward off the moral loss of being deemed racist. In this way, white knowledge of and literal or metaphorical proximity to non-white culture and non-white people becomes a means of acquiring moral capital.

The desire to learn is not white supremacist in and of itself. But patterns of "white talk" that seek to establish innocence through racial knowledge mediated by non-white people indicate that white ignorance can be *a need to know* as much as it can be a need *not* to know. In both cases, epistemology serves the interests of white moral benefit. As an industry has developed around anti-racist pedagogy, the denial tactics of "white talk" have become incorporated in claims to anti-racist pedagogy, anti-racism in the classroom, allyship, and institutional commitment to diversity. In Alison Jones's account of a classroom experiment with co-teacher and Maori scholar Kuni Jenkins, for example, we can see how white settler New Zealander students' desire to learn anti-racism with non-white Pacific Islander students "functioned to maintain the white students' self-image as "good"; but when the students of color 'snubbed the white students" well-intended desires for integrated discussion' about race, the white students expressed indignation 'instead of working to understand their role in the students" of color preference for separate classes. The white students were unaware but also unwilling to recognize that what they perceived as an empathetic desire functioned as a type of absolution.[26] In her study, Jones observes that white students" indignation could be attributed to their interpretation that students of color were "standing in their way of being 'good whites.'" It was more important, in other words, for white students to experience a process of racial absolution for themselves than to shift the racial power dynamics in the classroom. These classroom dynamics could be considered a microcosm of the role played by white ignorance in the dynamics of racial capitalism, since white negative affects of loss and aggrievement are directed at, and attributed to, non-white people as a way for white people to avoid the role of race and racism in their moral, material, and epistemic entitlements.

Jones characterizes her white students' resistance to recognizing the role of their desire for access as a "*refusal* to know" that manifests as "empathy," but which is in fact geared toward preserving moral rectitude. When Jones and Jenkins separated their students into ethnic groups part-time in response to the desires of students of color, white (or Pakeha[27]) students' "refusal to know" came through in their journals, as did the explicit recognition of students of color that having their own non-white classroom would allow them to avoid the emotional and epistemic labor demanded of them by white students invested in anti-racism. White/Pakeha students were almost uniformly unhappy about the classroom split and felt they had been "cheated" out of an educational opportunity, while segregation seemed to have the opposite effect for the Maori and Pacific Islander students who wrote in their journals that they felt more "confident," "less intimidated," and more "at ease." As one Pacific Islander student put it, "I felt as though I had moved towards the centre and stepped into the centre where white people normally reside. It felt good."[28]

While the white students in Jones and Jenkins's classroom meant to demonstrate their moral sensitivity through their attempts to educate themselves about racism, "their talk, instead, served to reproduce and maintain the culture of power in the classroom."[29] In Jones's analysis, the Pakeha students' anger and disappointment was prompted by their being denied the opportunity to be "good learners" in such a way that would grant them the experience of absolution. This white moral absolution requires access to, knowledge of, and epistemic and emotional labor on the part of students of color. It is in this sense that white ignorance has a moral economy.

New Zealand, like the US, is a settler colony, and Jones' attributes students entitlement to know and desire for dialogue to a "colonial romance" that, when thwarted, is expressed "in the annoyed words of the Pakeha students who felt cheated of such 'coming together.'"[30] The threat to "coming together" has "particular emotional force . . . because it is a threat to the dominant group at the very point of their power in education—their ability to *know*. A sense of exclusion and outrage marks the refusal of the already-privileged to accept that some knowledges and relationships might not be available to them/us."[31] Shannon Sullivan has called this solipsistic disposition "white ontological expansiveness," since it is an orientation that assumes that "all cultural and social spaces are potentially available" for one to inhabit, know, or "transact" with.[32]

White students were used to having a sense of "what there is to know," and confessions of ignorance as a desire to access that knowledge positioned them as "good students," curious to learn the "right" knowledge. The colonial, supremacist underpinnings of this desire to know/confession of ignorance are evident; Jones characterizes white students' entitlement as a "cannibal desire to 'know the other'" that is simultaneously a *refusal* to know. "It is a resistance to the possibility that the other cannot or might not want to be 'known' or consumed by them, or to teach them."[33]

In Jones's account, we can see that the students' white talk is centered on access to specialized knowledge, the desire for which white students take to demonstrate their racial goodness. The moral ecosystem here is a binary one, where white students seek to be "good" rather than "bad" whites, positioning non-white, colonized students as blameworthy when their own need to be recognized as "good" is disappointed. Their discursive distancing from their own complicity in racist dynamics is undertaken by both using and blaming non-white students. When access to knowledge is denied, the white students identify students of color as withholding racial redemption, echoing the legacies of colonial morality that reserved spiritual and moral authority and the tools of salvation for white settlers. As Jones writes of white students angry and "thwarted 'desire to know,'"

> The very act of 'knowing,' of 'being taught' becomes, most significantly, not an act of logic or an accumulation of information or even a call to action, but an *experience*: an experience of redemption. The Pakeha students' powerful and passive need for cleansing and absolution by the other is signaled by a panicked demand for it when it is not apparently forthcoming.[34]

"White talk"—whether it is a negative reaction to constructive criticism, or the resentment of white students rebuffed by students of color—serves to shield moral standing, often reinscribing and protecting whiteness "*even within attempts to disrupt its normative influence*" (emphasis in original).[35] These kinds of discourse that often show up in whites' interpersonal attempts to signal anti-racism indicate that white intention is not trustworthy as a barometer of moral success. Looking at white talk shows us that just as whiteness creates severe epistemic limitations, positioning white people to "see the world wrongly," it also shows the racial complicity of moral frameworks that prize individual intention over material impact, and moral standing over accountability for harm.

White readers will likely recognize some version of these tendencies in themselves, and far from indicting white people for their dismay and anger about the impact of racism, segregation, and colonization in their relationships with people of color, I have aimed to show the limitations of paradigms of responsibility that derive from settler moral economies. "White talk" that inoculates against the moral taint of racism is a structural phenomenon, linked to histories of appropriation and their religious and political justifications. It seeks moral relief in the face of realities that, if properly recognized, would threaten white moral and material benefit. The "white talk" of students seeking racial salvation through contact with non-white peers—an earnest, but unsuccessful attempt to respond to harm—shows us the limitations of notions of racial responsibility motivated by the pursuit of innocence. The remainder of this chapter finds this pattern at work in institutional declarations and apologies that, like Jones's white students, maintain power through selective, strategic contrition. Institutional declarations can function to deflect blame and preserve authority, participating in moral economies that reinforce white agency and normativity while obscuring the demands, resistance, and initiatives of people of color.

DEFLECTIVE DECLARATIONS: THE INOCULATING EFFECT OF INSTITUTIONAL COMMITMENT

In the summer of 2020, the institution where I teach discontinued the contract of the director of Emergency Management. Peter Amico, the fired employee, was a former police officer who had been hired as a security contractor by the university in 2008. In 1994, while on duty, Amico, who is white, had shot and killed El Tarmaine "L.T." Sanders, a Black teenager living in the same town as the university, after the boy's mother Delores Sanders called the police for help with a domestic violence incident. When Amico arrived on the scene and saw L.T. holding a knife, he immediately opened fire, claiming self-defense. Sanders was holding the knife because he had been fighting with his cousin, and his mother called the police for support in calming down the situation. Instead, Amico murdered her son. As James E. Johnson, an academic and organizer of the campaign for justice for El Tarmaine put it, "It was other-worldly, that Delores called police because her son was having a fight with his cousin and it seemed like, to us, that Amico just drove up there and shot L.T. without any kind of assessment of anything."[36]

Protests were held across the county in the months after the shooting. But heartbreakingly, and unsurprisingly, a federal investigation found "no civil rights violations" and a grand jury declined to bring charges against Amico. To add insult to injury, the Gloucester County Police Awards Committee gave Amico a Combat Cross award for "combat with an armed assailant"—14 year-old L.T.[37] Amico was not reprimanded, removed from duty, made to undergo bias training, or told he could no longer access a firearm—let alone indicted for murder. In fact, he suffered no legal or social consequences, and no economic consequences at the time; the judicial system not only came to his defense, but honored his behavior. This was only one example of an endemic refusal to hold whiteness to account in a country where policing normalizes and continues a racist history of armed white militias. It was also a consistent perpetuation of white ignorance for an institution of higher education ostensibly invested in "diversity" to hire Amico as a "security" contractor for young adults, who would then head the office of Emergency Management, an office whose mission is to "protect human life."

It took the murder of George Floyd and the mass movement to which it gave rise for the university to respond to the petition to fire Amico started by L.T.'s family (which garnered over 3500 signatures). Some in the university community criticized the university's timing, claiming that Amico's termination was a self-interested performance of racial accountability on the part of a neoliberal university concerned with maintaining its image. In a carefully worded statement, the college's president wrote, "As a University, we believe black lives matter. We are looking hard at our own organization, our policies, structure and culture. We found we have work to do. [. . .] We will be transparent in our transformation and look for opportunities to engage with the University community to bring about much-needed change."[38] The statement did not include an apology, or any indication of how the institution would go about undertaking such "much-needed change." Notably, the statement did not, outside the decision to discontinue his contract, take position on the wrongness of Amico's actions, and in a sympathetic gesture toward law enforcement, acknowledged "the difficulty police officers encounter" as a result of their "uncertain" job conditions and the "scrutiny" they face.[39] At first glance, this statement takes some responsibility for an atmosphere of structural racism in the action of dismissing an employee who engaged in racist police violence, and in claiming that it will do the "work" to make "needed changes." But on another register, such statements also do the "work" of inoculating an institution, and the individuals who move through it, from blame. This section looks at the ways that declarative responses to racism by white majority institutions use race, racism, and racial violence as the terrain for establishing moral goodness with respect to racial harm. Like white talk, institutional declarations serve to deflect from the ongoing racial harm built into the material operations of the university. Institutional declarations are crucial for understanding white ignorance, since they use race as a means to establish moral standing, all the while distancing racist incidents from the exploitative and extractive activities that are their raison d'être.

Amico's urgent dismissal twenty years after the event—too little accountability too late—bears a kind of metonymic relationship to other urgent efforts to address the irreparable harms of white supremacy. Many were politicized around race and white supremacy for the first time during the 2020 uprisings, and some long-time activists have expressed some cynicism about the urgency of newly politicized white people to do something immediate, claiming that such urgency to demonstrate anti-racism is an aspect of "white supremacy culture."[40] "What is underneath that urgent energy?" asks scholar and diversity worker Beth Berila. "What's underneath that righteous rage? Is it, at heart, a longing to be a good person? For people to *know* you are a good person?"[41] There is no question that the firing of Amico was meant to establish the institution as a "good" non-racist institution, ready to accept the tuition of non-white students. What is notable isn't just the fact of deflection, but that deflective declarations participate in neoliberal adaptations of settler moral economies that reproduce white moral capital through logics of absolution. That is, these statements function to generate moral and economic benefit on the fraught terrain of race. This means that those of us involved in anti-racism efforts in institutional spaces need to be wary of the ways that our work done in earnest can be taken up by logics of institutional innocence that use their moral capital to perpetuate racial capital, centering white normativity and profit at the expense of those who suffer its most negative impact.

"Diversity" is big business, and institutional efforts to address racism must contend with the fact that they participate in contexts governed by a neoliberal agenda of profit, commodification, and partnership with finance capital. In this context, declarations made by institutions in response to accusations of racism, according to M. Jacqui Alexander, tend to "manufacture consent and cohesion."[42] In her harrowing account of a collective mobilization to shift the whiteness and Eurocentrism of the New School for Social Research, Alexander writes that the timing of institutional diversity trainings and documents "can be seen as a gesture of consolidation" that positions faculty and students of color as additive numbers in a body count intended to manufacture a demographic constituency. The proximity of diversity declarations to crises in the institution's moral image "enables them to produce an impression of more 'diversity,' more 'radicalism,' than actually exists. . . .. Thus, they constitute the ideological work of representing representation."[43] Discourses of racial accountability and inclusion (broadly taken to be synonymous with diversity) are thus "deployed" as a kind of organized defense that "authorizes" the institution to maintain its structures of control and authority.[44] Such statements of commitment and accountability are morally ambiguous, since they can be used to exercise pressure on a university administration by holding it to its word, while also serving as an institutional technology that maintains dynamics of racial control by preserving its adjudicating role as the central moral agent. In this sense, institutional declarations of anti-racism, like "white talk," deflect responsibility while claiming to take it, protecting whiteness from the consequences of its own complicity.

Just as individuals signal their anti-racism in ways that reproduce racist dynamics by centering whiteness, institutions can maintain white normativity through the very act of acknowledging it. The declaration made in the wake of Peter Amico's firing, for example, acknowledged that "we have work to do."[45] Without apologizing directly, the institution is contrite; it believes that "black lives matter." In her work on institutional declarations of anti-racism in white-majority contexts, Sara Ahmed calls such statements of racial contrition "non-performative" insofar as they do not do what they say they do. Like white talk, they have an inoculating effect, where saying that one is "bad" is meant to indicate that a white person is "good" in their recognition of their complicity. In a similar vein, Fiona Probyn notes that white confession and anxiety for moral absolution is the very motor for "Critical Whiteness Studies," where a "good" disciplinary subject is created through the act of white acknowledgement.[46] Again, such a phenomenon isn't merely psychological, but a structural and political fixation on moral purification that protects white moral capital while allowing deeper patterns of inequality to go unchecked. The statement about Amico's firing, for example, set in motion a series of optional "diversity, equity, and inclusion" workshops meant to grant individual faculty racial knowledge without fundamentally changing the material relationships of white normativity on campus: the persistent whiteness of faculty and students with disproportionate racial diversity among contingent and lower-paid faculty, the racialization of staff in relation to faculty,[47] vocational programming focused on partnerships with extractivist business with ties to banking and finance, classroom and institutional environments that remain hostile to non-white students, and lack of accountability to communities of color living adjacent to the campus, where LT Sanders was murdered. According to Ariane Hutchins-Newman, declarations of accountability in the absence of plans for fundamental organizational change serve to "protect majority standing" not just because they serve to evade blame and encourage inaction, but because that pattern of evasion directly marginalizes non-whites for white material benefit.[48] In declaring the termination of Amico, the institution purified itself of moral taint, rehearsing a moral ritual that couches responsibility in terms of agents' ability to control their status as innocent or blameworthy through demonstrations of public contrition. This moral paradigm, as we have seen, isn't in conflict with histories of racial exploitation, but consistent and intertwined with it.

Where performative speech produces the effects that it names, non-performatives describe "practices by which discourse *does not produce* the effects that it names."[49] For Ahmed, examples of these "declarations of whiteness" include statements like "I/we are racist," "I/we are ashamed by my/our racism," "I/we have studied whiteness (and racist people are ignorant)," and "I am/we are [people of color] (too)."[50] In declarations like the one issued for Amico's dismissal, the college may well have intended its statements to function to create an atmosphere of anti-racism. Ahmed's insight is that beyond intention, we should focus on what such speech *does* or *does not do*. Not only do declarations of anti-racism frequently fail to do what they say they do; their manner of naming or self-describing, can, according to Ahmed, also be a way of *actively not bringing something into effect* in the very act of claiming accountability.

What is *not* brought into effect is the result of concerted, active habits that normalize white advantage, and it is in this sense that institutional declarations are an example of white ignorance. In the same way that white ignorance is a semi-willed set of habits that remains in place because of the moral, psychological and material benefits it confers, normalized institutional patterns can be thoughts of as "a continuation of willing what no longer needs to be willed."[51] While an institution may apologize for an acute, blameworthy action, capitalizing on it in order to frame itself as "cutting edge," institutional operations that preclude some possibilities while facilitating others, without explicit decisions needing to be made, continue unabated. White ignorance at the institutional level is highly motivated by the material benefits allowed by moral performance. While some of these declarative performances may be undertaken in bad faith, others might be sincere. What is salient, however, is the way that these rituals of moral purification serve to protect the extractive, accumulative operations of racial capitalism by focusing on collective or corporate moral status, rather than the conditions of racial harm.

Whether racism and white normativity are avowed or disavowed (and non-performatives can be either or both), non-performative declarations recenter white actions and white subjects, assuming that they can transcend the habits of the institutional body through aspirational talk or institutional "positive psychology."[52] Confessions of "bad practice" become, through the mechanics of the declaration, aspirational (but fantastical) indications of "good practice"; declarations of anti-racist commitment and "good practice" tend to evidence bad practice, insofar as the usual "commitments" – benchmarks, metrics, committees, trainings, numerical figures—become integrated into the habitual operations of the university with no follow-though.[53] Ahmed calls these declarative non-performatives "fantasies of transcendence," since they operate under the delusion that the declarations, confessions, and statements of commitment do the work of shifting racist dynamics. In fact, such confessions, declarations, statements, and commitments deflect from the material, organizational, and somatic changes that would have meaningful anti-racist impact. These kinds of declarations thus function as a need not to know that obfuscates, redirects, and deflects, shoring up individual and institutional status, while reproducing race-based material inequality.

Ahmed's analysis of the UK's 1999 MacPherson Report on racist policing is particularly helpful for identifying the risks inherent to anti-racist work in white-dominant institutions.[54] The MacPherson Report is notable for having recognized and established "institutional racism" as a problem within its organization, identifying racism as perpetuated unwittingly by "collectives" rather than individuals. The problem with the framing of institutional racism in the report, according to Ahmed, was that the report saw evidence of collective responsibility only in what those institutions "failed to do"; not in what it was actively *doing*, whether or not that doing was intended. Ahmed advocates instead for a definition of racism that would make it evident *not* "in what 'we' fail to do, but what 'we' have already done, whereby the 'we' is an effect of the doing."[55] The institutional confession of racism serves to immunize the police from charges of racist action, rather than recognizing the active habits, ways of being, institutional culture, and fundamentally racist history and *raisond'être* of the police.[56] [57]

A similar, seemingly paradoxical, deflection of responsibility is at work in public declarations of guilt, shame, and apology. In the last three decades, public apologies on the part of settler governments have been employed as an important technology of settler colonialism. While it is thought by many in settler colonies like Canada, Australia, and New Zealand that apologies for residential schools are an important "first step" on the road to forgiveness and reconciliation, Indigenous theorist Glenn Coulthard has shown the role that public apologies have in legitimating ongoing dispossession by locating colonial harm in the past. While post-war Truth and Reconciliation Commissions are transitional insofar as they are meant to usher a nation state into a new political reality in which damaged relationships are restored, the politics of reconciliation in settler colonies is "nontransitional," since settler colonialism is an ongoing, active set of processes. As Coulthard writes, in settler colonial contexts, "there is no period marking a clear or formal transition from an authoritarian past to a democratic present."[58] Public, state-sponsored projects of apology and reconciliation "must ideologically manufacture such a transition by allocating the abuses of settler colonization to the dustbins of history, and/or purposely disentangle processes of reconciliation from questions of settler-coloniality as such."[59] As forms of "conceptual obfuscation"[60] that reproduce racial-capitalism in the very moral discourses that claim to address it, public apologies that seek forgiveness without addressing the material circumstances of settler colonialism expose the moral dimension of white ignorance. Like the white aggrievement we saw in chapter 1, the settler logic of forgiveness that seeks to maintain and justify Indigenous dispossession along with the salvation of moral standing is a kind of hegemonic denial. Contemporary settler discourses of reconciliation and apology bear some similarity in structure and outcome to early Protestant discourses of "Christian Slavery," which sought to reconcile Protestant ideals of salvation and mastery with the ownership and exploitation of human beings by placing control of salvation and moral authority in the hands of white settlers. As Coulthard writes, reconciliation of Indigenous nationhood with the sovereignty of settler states "is still colonial insofar as it remains structurally committed to the dispossession of Indigenous peoples of our lands and self-determining authority."[61] The primary accumulation of settler colonialism is ongoing, and public apologies that do not address those material circumstances participate in perpetuating "moral non-knowings" that normalize and justify the ongoing genocide of Indigenous people.

The use of public apology as a technology of settler morality extends beyond the Canadian context. Sara Ahmed shows that in Australia's Sorry Books, an online repository of apologies for the colonial atrocities undergone by Australia's Indigenous population, expressions of white shame operate in such a way as to enshrine a national moral ideal that conceals the dispossession that is its condition of possibility. "National shame," Ahmed writes, "can be a mechanism for reconciliation as self-reconciliation, in which the 'wrong' that is committed provides the very grounds for claiming national identity. It is the declaration of shame that allows us 'to assert our identity as a nation,'" in a way analogous to the way that declarations of anti-racism assert a particular kind of white moral identity.[62] Recognition restores the nation and reconciles it to itself "by 'coming to terms with' its own past in the expression of 'bad feeling.' But in allowing apologizers to feel bad, shame also allows the nation *to feel better or even to feel good,*"[63] to feel "proud" of the ability to recognize and apologize for brutality. Because the apology indicates an overcoming of a racist nation and self assumed to exist now only in the past tense, it both supports racism in the present, and re-posits the white subject as the moral and social ideal. This morality of white settler self-reconciliation, rather than an antidote to colonial expropriation and violence, is consistent and supportive of it.

Not all declarations and apologies are instruments of colonial white supremacy. But institutions—universities, governments and government agencies, religious organizations, corporations—are important sites of normalization that are invested in the dynamics of the status quo. For this reason, institutional declarations of racial guilt or innocence are examples of white ignorance insofar as they simultaneously acknowledge and refuse to acknowledge participation in structural racism. The cases we saw above exemplify the conceptual and moral obfuscations of white ignorance: structural racism is acknowledged in order for its moral and political implications to be denied. This is the problem with frameworks of responsibility that limit their scope to determining the innocence or guilt of individuals and institutions, meting out punishment and absolution according to those determinations, while strategically deflecting away from the conditions that produce racial benefit and harm: racial-capitalism, settler colonialism, racialized relations of domestic and international extractivism and exploitation.

MORAL RESPONSIBILITY BEYOND THE WILL TO SAVE

This chapter looked at the patterns of moral benefit that perpetuate white ignorance even in—and because of—their attempts to absolve themselves of the charge of racism. White commitments and claims to anti-racism inhabit a seemingly paradoxical space, where the desire to be a "good" white person holds structures of white benefit in place, inhibiting the outcomes signaled by performances of accountability. What this shows is that the relentless focus on white moral status tends to re-center and re-feature whiteness and white moral capital, without necessarily shifting the everyday habits and patterns of inequality and dispossession that are the subject of declarations and statements.[64] The recognition of this very pattern of deflection is inhibited by a racial "need not to know" that maintains epistemic distance between white-positioned people and the understandings that might destabilize their everyday ways of being. That habitual racial ignorance might be only semi-conscious, or semi-willed, since it participates in long-standing moral economies that center white agency and tie it to an individual's capacity for salvation through thrift and work on God-given land. While historians and scholars have sought to qualify racial exploitation and white supremacy as distinct from, and condemnable by, the moral frameworks that developed during the colonial moment, I have argued here that Protestant moralities centered on an individual's elect status as "saved" were part of the racializing project of settlement, and continue to justify land dispossession, occupation, and exploitation today. That continuation of white saviorism doesn't merely uphold the status quo, but can result in violent repercussions for people of color. In the case of the protest described at the beginning of this chapter, the presence of a white-majority group of protesters was not simply an ideological and political reproduction of white moral authority. The use of non-white space for white anti-racist declarations increased the police presence, thereby increasing the likelihood of anti-Black police violence—the very thing being protested.

The implication of this critique of settler morality is not moral determinism, the idea that white morality has no choice but to necessarily embody these histories of supremacy. Gaining an understanding of the ways that white supremacy has shaped white moral inclinations and modalities of responsibility is necessary for moving through and beyond them toward a different notion of accountability centered on Black and non-white needs and demands. Critiques of white settler moralities based on agential mastery do not mean that the project of accountability and transformation should be abandoned, or that declarations, commitments, and apologies shouldn't be made. What it does mean is that these activities should be undertaken with an awareness of the motivational pull of white moral absolution and conservative draw of deflection that is a feature of white normativity. What we learn from looking at the moral economies at work in deflection and denial-through-admission is that alternative forms of accountability are needed that decenter white guilt and innocence. If we are going to destabilize white normativity, we need to become familiar with the ways that moral concepts and the behavior they justify, racial politics, and affect have conspired to create a paradigm of responsibility that, in centering guilt and innocence, limits our possibilities for confronting structural racism.

NOTES

1. Claudia Rankine, *The White Card* (New York: Graywolf Press, 2019), https://www.graywolfpress.org/books/white-card.
2. Uma Narayan, "Colonialism and Its Others: Considerations On Rights and Care Discourses," *Hypatia* 10, no. 2 (1995): 133–40.
3. Teju Cole, "The White-Savior Industrial Complex—The Atlantic," accessed May 26, 2021, https://www.theatlantic.com/international/archive/2012/03/the-white-savior-industrial-complex/254843/.
4. Philip L. Berg, "Racism and the Puritan Mind," *Phylon (1960)* 36, no. 1 (1975): 1–7, 1.
5. Ibid.
6. Ibid., 7.
7. Charles W. Mills, *The Racial Contract* (Cornell University Press, 2014).
8. Katharine Gerbner, *Christian Slavery: Conversion and Race in the Protestant Atlantic World* (University of Pennsylvania Press, 2018), 30.
9. Gerbner, 2.
10. Gerbner, 3.
11. Ibid., 11
12. Ibid.
13. Manisha Sinha, *The Slave's Cause: A History of Abolition* (Yale University Press, 2016).
14. Alana Massey, "The White Protestant Roots of American Racism," *The New Republic*, May 26, 2015, https://newrepublic.com/article/121901/white-protestant-roots-american-racism.
15. Ibid.
16. Sandra Lee Bartky, *Sympathy and Solidarity: And Other Essays* (Rowman & Littlefield, 2002); McIntyre in Barbara Applebaum, *Being White, Being Good: White Complicity, White Moral Responsibility, and Social Justice Pedagogy* (Lexington Books, 2010), 43.
17. Alison Bailey, "'White Talk' as a Barrier to Understanding Whiteness," in *White Self-Criticality Beyond Anti-Racism: How Does It Feel to Be a White Problem?*, ed. George Yancy (Lexington Books, 2014), 37–57, 39.
18. Ibid.
19. Ibid., 42.
20. Rachel McKinnon, "Allies Behaving Badly: Gaslighting as Epistemic Injustice," in *The Routledge Handbook of Epistemic Injustice* (Routledge, 2017), 8.
21. Nora Berenstain, "Epistemic Exploitation," *Ergo, an Open Access Journal of Philosophy* 3 (2016).
22. Applebaum, *Being White, Being Good,* 42.
23. Ibid., 43.
24. Ibid.
25. Ibid.
26. Applebaum, *Being White, Being Good*, 91.

27. "Pakeha" is the Maori word for foreigner, which has now come to mean white New Zealander or New Zealander of European descent.

28. Alison Jones, "Pedagogy by the Oppressed: The Limits of Classroom Dialogue," 1999, 8, https://www.aare.edu.au/data/publications/1999/jon99117.pdf., 2.

29. Applebaum, *Being White, Being Good*, 92.

30. Jones, "Pedagogy by the Oppressed: The Limits of Classroom Dialogue." 4.

31. Ibid.

32. Shannon Sullivan, *Revealing Whiteness: The Unconscious Habits of Racial Privilege* (Indiana University Press, 2006), 25.

33. Jones, "Pedagogy by the Oppressed: The Limits of Classroom Dialogue." 5.

34. Ibid.

35. Ibid.

36. Matt Gray, "Cop Who Shot and Killed Black N.J. Teen in 1994 Should Be Fired from University Post, Family Says," NJ.com, June 8, 2020, sec. Gloucester County, https://www.nj.com/gloucester-county/2020/06/cop-who-shot-and-killed-black-nj-teen-in-1994-should-be-fired-from-university-post-family-says.html.

37. Michael Tannenbaum, "Rowan University Drops Emergency Management Official Who Fatally Shot Teen in 1994 | PhillyVoice," accessed July 6, 2021, https://www.phillyvoice.com/rowan-university-peter-amico-eltarmaine-lt-sanders-shooting-1994-petition/.

38. Houshmand, "Acting in the Public Interest, Serving Public Trust," Rowan Today, June 8, 2020, https://today.rowan.edu/news/2020/06/acting-in-the-public-interest-serving-public-trust.html.

39. Ibid.

40. Kenneth Jones and Tema Okun, *Dismantling Racism: A Workbook for Social Change Groups* (Changework, 2001), https://resourcegeneration.org/wp-content/uploads/2018/01/2016-dRworks-workbook.pdf.

41. Beth Berila, "White Urgency to End Racism: Why Now?," *OpenDemocracy*, accessed July 6, 2021, https://www.opendemocracy.net/en/transformation/white-urgency-end-racism-why-now/.

42. M. Jacqui Alexander, *Pedagogies of Crossing: Meditations on Feminism, Sexual Politics, Memory, and the Sacred* (Duke University Press, 2006), 135.

43. Ibid.

44. Ibid., 137.

45. Houshmand, "Acting in the Public Interest, Serving Public Trust."

46. Fiona Probyn, "Playing Chicken at the Intersection: The White Critic of Whiteness," Borderlands E-Journal 13, no. 2 (2004).

47. Ariane Hutchins-Newman, "White Faculty Perceptions of Diversity and Diversity Work" (Glassboro, NJ: Rowan University, 2019), 167.

48. Ibid.

49. Sara Ahmed, *On Being Included: Racism and Diversity in Institutional Life* (Duke University Press, 2012).

50. Sara Ahmed, "Declarations of Whiteness: The Non-Performativity of Anti-Racism," *Borderlands* 3, no. 2 (2004), http://www.borderlands.net.au/vol3no2_2004/ahmed_declarations.htm.

51. Ahmed, *On Being Included.*

52. Ibid.

53. Ibid., 124.

54. Ahmed, "Declarations of Whiteness."

55. Ibid.

56. As Alex Vitale has shown, the police have their origins in British and US imperial control and occupation. The first police forces in the US and the UK were made to control poor and racialized people through armed violence, and to prevent labor organizing, and were modeled on the imperial occupying armies in places like the Philippines (in the case of the US). See Alex S. Vitale, *The End of Policing* (New York: Verso, 2017).

57. In her analysis of the MacPherson Report, Ahmed also alerts us to the fact that using the language of structural or institutional racism can deflect from the individual and micro-level motivations and actions that uphold racial inequality. As she writes, "the institution also *takes the place of individuals*: it is the institution that is the bad person, rather than this person or that person. In other words, the transformation of the collective into an individual (a collective without individuals) might allow individual actors to refuse responsibility for collective forms of racism" (Ibid.).

58. Glen Sean Coulthard, *Red Skin, White Masks: Rejecting the Colonial Politics of Recognition* (University of Minnesota Press, 2014), 108.

59. Ibid.

60. Ibid., 107.

61. Ibid., 151.

62. Ahmed, "Declarations of Whiteness," 11.

63. Ibid.

64. This is to say nothing of white public declarations of anti-racism that don't merely maintain a status quo, but that have direct negative, and sometimes violent, consequences for non-white people.

Chapter 3

Punitive Whiteness

Affective Economies of White Guilt and Shame

When radical left anti-capitalist discourse appears to align with conservative or right-wing ideas, there is always more to the story. The notion of white guilt is a site of such seeming alignment, with far-right and white nationalist groups declaring "No White Guilt," conservatives claiming that white guilt inhibits racialized groups from taking "personal responsibility,"[1] and voices on the left rejecting white guilt as associated with "oppressor consciousness"[2] or as self-centering at the expense of collective struggle. What is at stake in each case is the question of responsibility for racial harm: who has it, what they did or didn't do, what should or shouldn't be felt, and what reparation or response should or shouldn't follow. This chapter interrogates the role played by guilt, shame, and blame in addressing collective racial harm by looking at the function they play as an affective dimension of white ignorance.

Racial guilt, shame, and blame are highly politicized. White nationalist groups reject the notion of white guilt on the grounds that white people have nothing to feel or be guilty for. On their view, white people are entitled to their dominance, and are victims of immigration, Jews, the government, cultural loss, and therefore have no responsibility for racism. The white nationalist position goes so far as to claim that white people are the true victims of racial harm. Conservatives like Shelby Steele claim that white guilt is the attempt to recover moral authority after having lost it as a result of the civil rights movement.[3] For Steele, US policies of social support, affirmative action, and reparations, are driven by the white need for redemption for the sin of slavery, and have the paternalistic effect of "stealing agency" from Black people (a view that clearly neglects the continuing reality of racism post-1960s, and structural patterns and policies that have actively benefited white people as they disadvantage non-white and poor people). Like some on the left, Steele understands white guilt as an attempt to reestablish lost innocence. Left critiques of white guilt are also wary of its relationship to white innocence and moral authority, rejecting the notion that white feelings should be a priority in the project of racial justice. As Indigenous Action Media have written,

> Even if never admitted, guilt and shame generally function as motivators in the consciousness of an oppressor who realizes that they are operating on the wrong side. While guilt and shame are powerful emotions, think about what you're doing before you make another community's struggle into your therapy session. Of course, acts of resistance and liberation can be healing, but tackling guilt, shame, and other trauma requires a much different focus, or at least an explicit and consensual focus. What kinds of relationships are built on guilt and shame?[4]

To elide the conservative and left framings would be to ignore the fact that where the conservative critique put forward by Steele is meant to shore up an individualist, capitalist discourse of personal responsibility, critiques from the left mean to expand responsibility and accountability beyond the personal, to encompass material conditions of inequality. While on first glance these discourses might seem to align, on further inspection we can see that the conservative account is premised on the false notion that because institutional racism ended with the "great confession" of the 1960s, white responsibility can only belittle Black people with welfare when it should instead promote bootstraps personal responsibility under a status quo assumed to be just and fair. Left anti-racist critiques, however, do not assume a just and fair world. Rather, they take white guilt to be implicated in a set of ongoing unjust power dynamics and material inequalities that are perpetuated through white habits and affects.

Progressive and left discussions of guilt and shame still struggle, however, with the place of these affects. On the one hand, actions motivated by white guilt and shame can limit the scope of anti-racist action by keeping it within the bounds of white emotional comfort and safety, prioritizing white agency and moral standing at the expense of the goals, needs, histories, and movements of people of color. White guilt that needs to be urgently relieved can propel white people into leadership roles that reproduce white power and authority, even in the effort to shift racist patterns. Guilt and shame can also be great inhibitors: as Ruth Frankenburg showed in the 1980s, the desire for racial absolution can be paralyzing for white people who retreat from anti-racist efforts out of fear that they will "mess up."[5] On the other hand, guilt and shame can catalyze accountability. White people *should* have negative feelings about their participation in racism, and should be motivated by those feelings to act. *Over*-critiquing guilt and shame can likewise lead to paralysis, or worse, to apathy, disconnection, and abdication of responsibility.

Some might claim that white ignorance is a deficiency of guilt and shame, a refusal to face what is disturbing and the negative affects that should accompany its recognition.

If both of these approaches to racial guilt seem true—that it is both motivating and inhibiting, both self-centering and self-correcting—it is because the psychological function of racial guilt and shame is not well understood.[6] Guilt and shame are difficult to measure and distinguish, as is the relationship between feeling guilty and collective guilt. Recent psychological studies on white guilt and shame do seem to indicate that feelings of guilt tend to be accompanied by a desire for "corrective" behavior. But little has been concluded about the relationship between feelings of guilt for collective racial harm and anti-racist action. This is because other factors intervene; as we will see, feelings of guilt have been shown by psychologists to have different impacts depending on other emotional and ideological variables. Guilt and shame are not-free floating, isolatable feelings, but are deeply connected to group belonging, relationships, self-concept, ideology, concepts of responsibility, and the consequences of transgressing rules, norms, and standards. The functions and roles played by racial guilt and shame, then, are difficult to understand without reference to their political context and political function.

White affects of guilt and shame in response to participation racial harm cannot be separated from the political and moral economies we saw in chapters 1 and 2. This chapter thus considers racial guilt, shame, blame, and punishment in the context of white supremacy and racial capitalism. Where chapter 2 focused on the way that moral concepts participate in exploitation and dispossession, this chapter looks at the way that affect is conscripted in the project of white denial and deflection. I argue that affect has an important role in perpetuating white ignorance by contributing to binary, racialized notions of guilt and innocence that associate "right feeling" to attributions of civic and civil status. Demonstrating the correct kind of affect and sensitivity has been used in the US to demarcate criminality. Where chapter 2 established that moral innocence and salvation is raced, this chapter establishes affective guilt and innocence as raced in an economy of feeling where good whiteness aims to avoid and displace punishment and blame. That avoidance, as we have seen thus far, is a core process in upholding white supremacy.

If the psychological functions of guilt and shame are ambiguous and difficult to generalize, the societal impact of our approaches to transgressing rules and norms is easy to observe. As the most punitive and incarcerating society in the world, the US is clearly preoccupied with questions of guilt and innocence as indicators of moral and civic status. This chapter is interested in the ways that guilt and shame circulate to establish racialized patterns of belonging, moral worth, and sensitivity on the one hand, and rejection and immutable punishability on the other hand. Chapter 2 argued that moralities centered on moral absolution are complicit in the consolidation of settler states through their linking of whiteness with spiritual and racial mastery. Because of this entanglement, white anti-racism in settler contexts participates in a moral economy that tends to reward white goodness, even when white people attempt to destabilize it. Where that chapter focused on the problem of mastery and moral standing rooted in slavery and colonialism, this chapter situates racial guilt and shame within the punitive affective economies of the US. Rather than rejecting white guilt and shame outright, I outline their ambiguities and limitations by looking at the ways these affects are racialized—the way that expressions of guilt and shame are complicit in racialized processes of belonging. As Paula Ioanide has written, "emotional rewards and losses play a central role in shaping how and why people invest in racism, nativism, and imperialism in the US."[7] Emotions are not merely personal or individual, but, like economies, "have mechanisms of circulation, accumulation, expression, and exchange that give them cultural legibility and political power."[8] Thus, this chapter asks: What affective racial economies make guilt and shame what they are to us, and what, in turn, do guilt and shame accomplish through race?

This chapter begins by discussing the most recent psychological research on guilt and shame. I show that the ambiguous role of both of these affects results from the difficulty of establishing causality and intention with respect to institutional or collective harm. This is to say that the effectiveness of racial guilt and shame in motivating white anti-racism is flexible because when guilt and shame are "collective," they are implicated in broader political patterns beyond conscious will and intention. Because guilt and shame are connected to the pre-conscious processes of denial at work in white ignorance, the feelings and dispositions we associate with responsibility are implicated in the process of racialization. To focus our studies of guilt and shame only on individuals' awareness and acknowledgment of racism ignores preconscious, political function of these affects. For that reason, I turn to affect theory and political theory to fill in the gaps. I show that, while guilt and shame may be galvanizing for some to take anti-racist action, these affects are not separable from a punishment paradigm that took root in the US during the nineteenth century. In this punishment paradigm, guilt, shame, and innocence were, and still are, raced. As Toni Morrison writes, our moral concepts are not detachable from racial difference and racial violence. Many might want to claim that

> white America has considered questions of morality and ethics, the supremacy of mind and the vulnerability of the body, the blessings and liabilities of progress and modernity, without reference to the situation of its black population. After all, it will be argued, where does one find a fulsome record that such

a referent was part of these deliberations? My answer to these questions is another: where is it not?[9]

If white ignorance inhabits the moral paradigms by which we respond to harm, we urgently need to understand how. This chapter demonstrates that the punitiveness of raced moralities demands a different, more accountable orientation toward collective white harm. While guilt and shame are indeed powerful and sometimes motivating affects, understanding their relationship to racialization can help us determine how to approach or distance ourselves from them in the process of confronting white supremacy.

THE AMBIGUITIES OF GUILT AND SHAME

Guilt and shame are natural reactions for white people to have as a response to their increasing awareness of the ongoing violence of whiteness and white supremacy. While the desire for moral absolution can be a barrier to effectively shifting white ignorance, as we saw in chapter 2, guilt and shame are feelings that should be expected when white people recognize their role in causing harm. Psychologist Corinne Galgay takes contemporary racial guilt and shame to reflect a shift in the nature of racism from more overt to more "covert," as well as "the changing nature of racial discourse in society, whereby whites' dominant status is no longer ignored and unchallenged."[10] The hegemonic denials of white ignorance are defensive reactions to challenges to white dominance and benefit, emotional responses to being "recognized as a racial being."[11] While these affects are said to be "negative" insofar as they are associated with distressing or uncomfortable emotions, some have discussed them as "dynamic" states that can lead to positive change. As Linda Alcoff has written, "the anger that shame and guilt evokes is justified and can be politically productive when directed toward the real causes of our unwitting complicity."[12] Researchers are divided, however, on how to label the range of negative emotions elicited when white people are confronted with their participation in racist systems, and to what extent these emotional reactions are involved in "corrective" behavior, support for racial justice policies, or their obverse. Looking at this research is important for developing realistic responses to racism and the white denial, dominance, and deflection that are central to its perpetuation. It also helps us see the insufficiency of guilt and blame based moral paradigms for addressing collective racial harm that may not have been originally caused or intended by contemporary white individuals, but in which they participate, and from which they benefit.

The emotional states of shame and guilt are rooted in the need for connection and belonging, and the fear of breaking rules or codes that might separate one from others. Guilt tends to be understood as an expression of one's *having done* wrong—having committed an act that violates a set of rules or norms—whereas shame is an expression of one's *being* wrong.[13] According to some researchers, guilt is act-focused and other-regarding, whereas shame is self-regarding. On this view, guilt can be understood as a fear of real or imagined punishment for transgressing a rule or law (self or other imposed), and shame can be understood as a reaction to the exposure of an aspect of oneself considered undesirable.[14] When one is in the affective state of guilt, "one negatively appraises one's behavior as transgressing a norm to which one adheres."[15] In shame, "one is in a distinctive emotional relation to oneself, which one appraises as globally negative. The self is appraised as degraded or worthless."[16]

Guilt is generally understood to be associated with adaptive, "compensatory action," while shame is understood to be maladaptive, related to feelings of fear, frustration, and helplessness. Criminal justice advocate Danielle Sered has argued that shame is not only inhibits accountability, but tends to lead to cycles of violence, isolation, and fear.[17] This is consistent with psychologist Brené Brown's contention that guilt can be more helpful for addressing racist harm than shame, which disparages an actor's self-worth, triggering a fight, flight or freeze response.[18] Where guilt can help white people detach their own worth from their actions in order to take accountability for them, "shame is not an effective social justice tool. Period. Shame," Brown writes, "is a tool of oppression."[19] According to Brown, shame is paralyzing, engaging the limbic system in defense responses to threat that make it difficult for the "thinking brain" to get back "online," whereas guilt allows for harm to be acknowledged and accounted for with less pain and dissociation. Guilt, in other words, can be helpful for addressing racial harm. As an affect that accompanies the recognition that an act has violated one's principles and commitments, guilt could be understood as the condition for apology and repair when an instance of white ignorance has occurred. Shame, however, could be understood as counterproductive since it participates in racist logics that evaluate human beings as globally good or bad.

But some researchers have troubled any clean distinctions we might want to make between these two affective states, as well as their respective orientations toward "self" or "other," especially in the context of race and racism. This is because racial guilt and shame rarely occur in isolation, since awareness of racial harm necessarily involves the tension between harmful realities and white self-concept.[20] In their research on the "psychosocial costs of racism for whites," Spanierman and Heppner find that white guilt and shame tend to exist in feedback loops, with affect shifting as racial awareness increases: recognition that one has participated in racial harm on account of being white has been observed to manifest as both guilt and shame.[21] Others find that white guilt and shame cannot be measured with a single-scale score outside of a "cluster analysis" that takes empathy, fear, and "multicultural awareness" into account[22]—factors that fall outside of the distinctions between "self" and "other" regard. The fear that accompanies racial awareness may also be an expression of shame. For this reason, guilt and shame have been theorized by psychologists as belonging to a cluster of negative affects that includes isolation, hopelessness, anxiety, frustration, loss, fear, low self-esteem, and a distorted sense of danger[23]—with lukewarm results for motivating anti-racist behavior when they are taken on their own. Because contemporary moral discourse on whiteness—particularly between white people—tends to be experienced as guilt and shame-inducing, the project of mitigating the harm of white ignorance demands a closer look at the role these affects play, and the extent to which they participate in reproducing it.

THE MOTIVATIONAL LIMITS OF GUILT AND SHAME

If the distinction between guilt and shame is ambiguous, so is the role that both of these negative emotions play when it comes to motivating action in response to racial awareness. In studies of restorative justice processes, guilt has been related to "taking responsibility" insofar as it motivates a person who engaged in harm to "confess, apologize, or repair."[24] Others, however, take shame to be more effective, since it calls a person's integrity and sense of self into question. In *Black Power: The Politics of Liberation*, for example, Kwame Ture and Charles V. Hamilton endorse white shame as a transformative force. "Can a man condemn himself? Can whites, particularly liberal whites, condemn themselves?" they ask. "Can they stop blaming blacks and start blaming their own system? Are they capable of the shame which might become a revolutionary emotion? We—black people—have found that they usually cannot condemn themselves; therefore black Americans must do it."[25] The transformative power of white shame is also taken up by philosopher Dan Haggerty, who argues that shame should be cultivated by white people in response to structural racism: their whiteness—*who and what they are*—is a harm to account for and to address. If shame is a personal experience of appraisal where our character and our ability to live in community with others are evaluated, then there is promise in shame and shaming: white people *should* be concerned with the problem of what they are, and should reckon with the ways that whiteness has fundamentally structured their habits and self-conceptions (Haggerty 2009, 306). His view echoes that of Bernard Williams, who understands shame to be more responsive to the fear of losing community and belonging than guilt. If shame is fundamentally about cultivating the right character in response to problems in our own communities and selves, it could be argued that it is an appropriate response to white ignorance.

But some studies paint a different picture that calls into question the effectiveness of guilt and shame in addressing racial harm. In the context of restorative justice processes, guilt has been shown to elicit "counterproductive resentment" and "chronic guilt," that is, guilt that becomes a disposition.[26] In this respect guilt becomes difficult to dissociate from the paralyzing effects of shame. White guilt and shame have been shown by psychologists to have an ambiguous status with respect to anti-racism, at times motivating learning and action, and at other times prompting denial, avoidance, and aggression.[27] Guilt and shame together can be associated with personal transformation and accountability, but are equally likely to coincide with "dysfunctional rescuing, paternalistic attitudes towards people of color as well as avoidance of racial content that may be interpreted as racist."[28]

Even without looking to the political functions of expressions of guilt and shame that we saw in chapter 2, psychological studies alone give us good reasons to be circumspect about their transformative power. While guilt might have seemed promising for promoting anti-racism, it seems to be the most effective in responding to harm when it can be "alleviated through behavioral patterns"—when the "offending act" can be repaired with specific, identifiable, targeted actions that respond directly to the harm caused.[29] Guilt that cannot attach itself to a particular reparable act is what some have called "chronic guilt" or "collective guilt."[30] The affect of racial guilt could be considered chronic insofar as no single action by any individual can "alleviate" the problem that gives rise to the feeling. We can see here that psychologizations of racial harm lead to ambiguity and non-answers, precisely because moralities of individual guilt, shame, and blame are not adequate responses to collective racial harm. The contradictory results of psychological studies of racial affect show us that guilt and shame run the risk of perpetuating denial, avoidance, and victimization narratives. Thus, we have good reason to be wary of them as responses to forms of structural, collective harm like white ignorance.

REPAIRING RACIAL IDENTITY OVER REDRESSING RACIAL HARM

As wide ranging as the results of psychological studies are, the desire to alleviate negative affect seems to be what is most consistent in studies of guilt and shame. We have seen in this chapter that some emphasize the self-punishing function of guilt, while others emphasize its pro-social, reparatory function. Still, even some of those in the latter category have found that reparation only serves to "assuage doubts of one's egalitarianism"—that is, doubts that one has discriminatory or problematic views.[31] Approaches to anti-racism wrestle with this problem, since white people are primed to want to relieve these negative affects because of the normativity of white ignorance. Guilt and shame-inducing political education is common, and has the added function of shoring up the self-regard of those who see themselves as more advanced in racial knowledge.

The implications of psychological research on guilt and shame that shows them to motivate the "assuaging of doubts" about one's moral status is that they do little to destabilize long-standing historic patterns of white claims to moral absolution and mastery. In studying what motivates people to change their behavior, researchers Amodio, Devine and Harmon-Jones found that when white research subjects with "egalitarian views" were given "bogus results" of their own brain scans which falsely indicated racial bias, those who presented brain scan signs of guilt tended, after a period of downtime, to choose pieces of writing on topics like "unlearning racial bias." This could be considered "other-regarding" in the sense that subjects were motivated to *educate* themselves on how to shift their racial bias. But it is unclear whether their study implies that these same research subjects would shift their interpersonal behavior beyond knowledge acquisition and the minimum actions required in order not to be considered racist in the eyes of others. Indeed, they are not the only researchers who have shown that what is at stake in white experiences of guilt and shame is self-concept, approval, and avoidance of punishment, rather than a meaningful or consistent commitment to anti-racism. Swim and Miller, for example, found that white guilt "reflects personal feelings about being white" rather than feelings of "racial inequity";[32] in another study, Tracy and Robins found that "guilt and shame" are only elicited when events were interpreted as "relevant" to one's "identity or self-representation."[33] The desire to maintain a particular kind of racial identity and sense of self intervened in how moral affect was taken up.

Because of their observed relationship to preserving self-concept, white guilt and shame are not effective for motivating responses to collective harm. Rather, feelings associated with collective guilt have been shown to motivate punishment, the desire to "let others know" that they are wrong, rather than to engage in actions that would address the harm.[34] As Galgay writes, "those that experience white guilt may be driven to make amends in order to avoid anger by the target and preserve positive self-image. This focus would impair, rather than foster, other-oriented empathy, and leave the target holding the burden to assuage the white individual's guilt."[35]

There isn't much evidence, then, to support the connection between guilt and shame and anti-racist action. In fact, the contrary seems to be true: guilt and shame seem to motivate the alleviation of negative affect as quickly as possible, while diverting blame onto others along the way. Guilt and shame based frameworks of responsibility encourage white exceptionalism—a project of absolving oneself of the incontrovertible personal badness of whiteness by rejecting white identity, while castigating others. The project of dispelling the negative affects associated with being white, rather than the structures that produce white benefit, encourages versions of anti-racism that prioritize "letting others know" in order to establish relative white goodness. As we saw with liberal racism in chapter 1, this project of dispelling negative affect and dissociating oneself from the identities associated with racial harm is undertaken at the expense of those who are working class, poor, or uneducated. Those considered "bad whites," the others who must be "let know" about their racism, serve to relieve "good whites" of their negative affect and responsibility for perpetuating racism.[36] This dynamic of "letting others know" does little to address one's own participation in racism, since it seeks to relieve individual white people of the threat of punishment, focusing on a personal "unlearning" and projection onto others rather than on the collective actions required to change social conditions. In this sense, guilt and shame participate in the perpetuation of white ignorance, rather than being an adequate moral corrective.[37]

Psychological studies of guilt and shame tend to assume a framework of responsibility that takes "personal awareness," intention, and avowed causality as indicators of accountability. Some studies could measure feelings of remorse, but none could establish a connection between feelings of remorse about white benefit and corrective actions beyond self-education and "letting others know" that they were in the wrong. Individuals were shown to have little motivation to act when their own identities were not at stake; awareness, guilt, and shame did not necessarily motivate a change in behavior, especially normalized, socially sanctioned behaviors. What this shows is that while guilt and shame can have an important role for some, they only do because other political, social, and material relations are at work. That is, guilt and shame do not, on their own, produce commitments to anti-racism, and are complicit in the reproduction of the denials and deflections of white ignorance. Affective guilt and shame, detached from the institutions and forms of power that give them context, will necessarily be inadequate for addressing collective harm. Focusing primarily on feelings and personal awareness while ignoring the role of power relations and economic exploitation contributes to a depoliticizing of anti-racism that allows its conditions to persist.[38] As we have seen, structural racism and its persistence are not simply the result of the attitudes, biases, and prejudices of individuals. If anti-racist education does not address factors beyond individual attitude, causality, and intention, then it will only reproduce patterns of white deflection motivated by the desire not to be punished, and to relieve the negative affects of guilt and shame by punishing others. This supports the idea that white anti-racism needs a moral paradigm beyond guilt and shame, beyond the racialized meting out of punishment and absolution. This alternative moral paradigm will need to address the ways that state institutions reinforce racialized binaries of guilt and innocence. Thus, the remainder of this chapter makes the difficult but important connection between white affective guilt and the maintenance of white innocence through punitive state institutions that reinforce a raced concept of "personal responsibility."

PUNITIVE WHITENESS AND CIVILIZED AFFECT

If guilt and shame are fundamentally about valuations of what is relevant for one's identity, group belonging, protection from racial discomfort, and negative self-conceptions, then they cannot avoid being implicated in collective processes of racialization. Expressions and cultivations of white guilt and shame are politically ambiguous because white moral feeling is caught up in the psychic wages of whiteness—the emotional and moral benefits that white people, across classes, access on account of race. It is true that these emotions may be necessary, to a degree, in moving white people toward accountability. But it is also true that they are part of an old US dynamic where affect and sensitivity with respect to race are employed in the service of creating and maintaining, rather than challenging, racial hierarchies. In this dynamic, guilt and shame, innocence and blame, are entangled with the racialization of punishability and civilizability. As we have seen, psychological studies of guilt and shame show that the anti-racism they motivate is primarily about dispelling negative affect, establishing "good" anti-racist identity, and "letting others know" that they are racist, rather than engaging in personal transformation or the transformation of material circumstances.

The backdrop for these psychological tendencies is what Mujahid Farid has called the "punishment paradigm."[39] The punishment paradigm is a social, moral, and political framework rooted in retributive conceptions of justice and colonial processes of racialization that responds to harm and violence with more harm and violence. The term was developed by criminal justice advocates to identify the ways that punitive responses to harm contribute to racism, racialization, and racist exclusion. According to critics of the punishment paradigm, the persistence of racism in society cannot be disconnected from the divestment of resources from racialized communities, who, as a result, are over-criminalized and over-incarcerated as a means of racialization. These punitive frameworks contribute to racialization by penalizing poverty as an individual failing, and racializing that divestment through criminalization. By deflecting away from material divestment, internal colonization,[40] and hyperexploitation, the punishment paradigm is a form of white ignorance. White ignorance perpetuates racial harm by deflecting away from its root causes and dynamics, denying participation in structures of racial benefit by individualizing racism. White guilt and shame are not the direct causes of structural racism, but insofar as they participate in the dynamics of deflection and white emotional relief, they maintain the conditions of racial harm.

Avoidance of the collective dimension of racism encourages a focus on white feelings of goodness, moral relief, and absolution that are historically linked to the punishment and exclusion of non-white people. It is in this sense that white racial guilt and shame—and the desire for relief, forgiveness, and the restoration of innocence that accompany them—participate in an affective economy of white ignorance. That affective economy has its roots in nineteenth century processes of racialization that associated the innocence and goodness of whiteness with individuals' ability to express emotion in the "right" way. As Kyla Schuller writes in *The Biopolitics of Feeling*, the capacity for cultivating and integrating the "right feeling" with respect to evocative experiences—what she calls "impressibility"—was understood by proponents of nineteenth century racial science not just as an appropriate guide to political action, but an indication of the supremacy of white civilization.[41] Schuller writes that at the height of the consolidation of the US as an industrializing nation state built on the stolen land, bodies, and labor of non-white people, "civilization" originated in the faculty of sentiment, granting "civilized" individuals control over their own evolution. Impressibility—the ability to be correctly affected—and sentiment became "the material basis of race, the criteria by which members of the population were determined to be an asset to the whole whose life should be enhanced, or a threat to its flourishing who must be disposed."[42] Sensitivity, according to Schuller, "connotes both the capacity for growth and the possession of nervous 'susceptibility,' a characteristic allegedly overdeveloped among wealthier women."[43] In other words, emotional sensitivity and expressed vulnerability—an attunement, management, and delicate integration of feelings—demonstrates one's status as civilized, or at least civilizable. Vulnerability and susceptibility are relational markers that demarcate whiteness as something to be protected and defended, and white emotional expressions in response to racial discomfort as raced, gendered, and classed.

The cultivation and expression of white moral sensitivity is not only understood in Schuller's research as a normative response to racial difference; it plays an integral role in constructing racial difference itself, establishing sensitive whiteness as a civilizational paradigm, in tension with and opposition to its non-white, insensitive, impervious counterpart. Nineteenth century whiteness, in other words, constructed itself through the threat of a racialized and less civilized other, who inspired fear, benevolence, and violence all at once. This is notably similar to contemporary expressions of white tears, which Damon Young and Mamta Motwani Accapadi have described, respectively, as "obliviousness, defensiveness, hypersensitivity, narcissism, [and] fabricated persecution,"[44] and "resistance" to difficult dialogue about privilege by seeming "helpless" or "innocent."[45] Schuller's work gives historical context for such counter-productive, deflective outbursts of moral feeling, tying them to nineteenth century white nation-building efforts. These efforts relied on fabricated racial differentiations based on the presumed capacity to absorb and express emotional input: white Anglo-Saxons had a hereditary ability to "discipline the body's impressibility, and thus evolutionary development, through self-control," whereas racialized others required benevolent assistance from whites, whose "right feelings" and sensitive negative affect were understood as tantamount to civic engagement. This "scientific" view of the civilizing role of sentiment in determining who is eliminatable, in combination with the Protestant work ethic, can help us understand the origins of a continuing dynamic that sets the stage for white negative affect that is at once defensive, deflectionary, benevolent, morally outraged, and emotionally responsive (though not materially responsible!) with respect to racial harm.

This is not to say that white people should not feel guilt and shame, or should be "insensitive" to negative feelings that arise as a result of their participation in racial harm. Sandra Bartky has argued that castigating white people for feeling guilty is anti-feminist and masculinist, insofar as it sets an unrealistic, unfeeling, and patriarchal standard of "hardness" in social movement culture.[46] While acknowledging the importance of this critique, we can also examine the conditions that make affective expressions like white tears a manifestation of racial power. To take such reactions to be tantamount to a desire for racial accountability shows us the limitations of notions of white responsibility premised on individuals' conscious intention and sense of self, rather than what would be required to end white material and moral dominance. Schuller's account is not critical of emotions per se, but shows how white affect was involved in the process of racialization from the beginning.

The affective economy of white guilt and shame described by Schuller is meant to describe realities beyond their nineteenth-century consolidation. Nineteenth-century distinctions—between sensitive, morally affected, white citizens measured against a non-white source of negative affect and civilizational threat—are evident in the racialization and institutionalization of punishment in the US. The continuity is clear: almost all parts of the criminal punishment system in the US are geared toward perpetual punishment rather than rehabilitation, indicating that overrepresented racialized groups are not sensitive or civilizable enough to live independently of those punitive institutions. Meanwhile, white reactivity rarely results in punishment and rarely engenders consequences that might modify behavior, as we saw with the firing of Peter Amico in chapter 2. The lack of accountability for the murder of unarmed non-white people by armed white people acting on their feelings of racial threat is a particularly salient and heartbreaking example. White reaction protects the vulnerability and innocence of white civilization, locating the source of harm, violence, and wrong among uncivilizable, racialized others.

The affective economies described by Schuller can help explain the extreme punitiveness of white US society. US white people are among the most punitive in the world, as a result of the racialization of guilt and innocence.[47] A recent report on punitiveness among white people conducted by the Sentencing Project not only shows the violent impact of prioritizing white evaluations of safety; it also shows how racialized perceptions of crime and innocence are linked to notions of responsibility. White moral affect plays a role in distributing punishability and eliminatability: The populations targeted by the hyper-punitive systems and institutions at work in the contemporary United States clearly show who is given the luxury of feeling, contemplating, and expressing their own participation in harm, and who is locked up with no second chances, or otherwise eliminated (through police or white vigilante murder, deportation, or lack of access to the necessities of life). At the core of this societal dynamic is the aggressive enforcement of whiteness—white people, white institutions, white society—as innocent, even as (and precisely because) the threat of being exposed as otherwise looms as white settler populations feel their demographic dominance to be threatened.

The Sentencing Project report cites studies that demonstrate the links between "racial perceptions of crime and punitive policy preferences."[48] In these studies, they found that "whites—though not blacks and Hispanics—who attributed higher proportions of violent crime, burglary, or robbery to blacks were significantly more likely" to have a preference for policies including "'making sentencing more severe for all crimes,' 'executing more murderers,' 'making prisoners work on chain gangs,' 'taking away television and recreation privileges from prisoners,' and 'locking up more juvenile offenders.'"[49] Strikingly, this relationship remained statistically significant even when the researchers controlled for other factors related to punitiveness *including* racial prejudice, conservatism, crime salience, and residence in the South.[50] Whiteness was the consistent predictor of punitiveness, even for those with no avowed racial prejudice—people who might have been determined "anti-racist" in the psychological studies cited earlier in this chapter. The report shows that punitive responses to harm are linked with denial and deflection with respect to race, since they document a white investment to define itself against harmful acts. If harm and wrong are racialized, then whiteness can deny its own participation in racism. This is practically a textbook definition of the problem of white ignorance that aggressively defends its racial innocence by shunting blame onto racialized others.

The report also found that whites who agreed that "African Americans pose a greater threat to public order and safety than other groups" were significantly more likely to hold punitive views in general than those who did not, and that this pattern did not hold for other racial groups. The same held true for juvenile justice: when these researchers analyzed a 2010 survey, they found that racialized views of youth crime and victimization "led whites, but not blacks, to support punitive juvenile justice policies."[51] These researchers concluded, referencing whites' concurrent "support for child saving" documented by the report, that "public support for punitive juvenile justice policies represents a desire to control other people's children."[52] In other words, punitiveness, the racialization of crime, and benevolent/paternalistic racist control were found to overlap with whiteness. For the authors of the report, the "weight" of the evidence suggests that "people with racial associations of crime"—a category in which whites were overrepresented—are more punitive regardless of whether they are overtly racially prejudiced." This is to say that whiteness and racial associations with criminality were enough to predict a punitive orientation toward harm. In turn, punitive orientations toward harm focus on individualizable, isolatable, instances of harm rather than the conditions that produce harm.

This is of course not to say that all white people are necessarily punitive as a matter of racial essence, or that only white people are. The statistical tendencies, however, do corroborate the way that white punitiveness, denial of the material conditions of harm, and political belonging in the project of nation-formation are of a piece. Punishment tends to be criminalized only when it doesn't apply to white bodies and selves. As Schuller shows in her work, nation-building ideologies and scientific racism in the nineteenth century distinguished between civilizable bodies, which could be controlled and managed by white minds, and those bodies that were uncivilizable and unmanageable, and therefore needed the external support of white authority and white institutions to modify behavior. The statistical reality of white punitiveness speaks to the fact that white moral responsibility has historically been associated with the constructed notions of individual self-control, self-governance, and self-management, and non-whiteness with the absence of those capacities. While this is clearly a racist reversal of the actuality of white impulsiveness, reactivity, and pre-conscious defensiveness, this discourse shows us how affective expressions of guilt and shame are involved in punitive notions of responsibility that position white people as conscious actors, whose innocent sensitivity should elicit sympathy and forgiveness from (non-white) others. This kind of reversal is a clear example of the affective dimension of white ignorance, and the hold that it has had on our notions of responsibility.

This impact of white affect on notions of responsibility shines through in the Sentencing Project report. The authors find a direct connection between punitive whiteness and individualistic notions of responsibility, citing that (1) "whites have fewer and more positive encounters with police and courts relative to racial minorities" and as a result perceive themselves as more "law abiding," responsible citizens; (2) whites are more likely to harbor and express overt and less overt racial prejudice; and (3) white Americans have a greater likelihood to "attribute criminal behavior to individual failure, rather than to contextual causes."[53] Crucially, this punitiveness is framed as a kind of inconsistency similar to the denial we saw in chapter 1. The report notes that "the prevalence of lingering prejudices and the reluctance to acknowledge structural racism creates a schism for many whites between widely-held egalitarian principles and support for policies to address racial gaps."[54] An earlier report, for example, showed that "the majority of whites attributed the black-white economic inequality during the late 1990s to individualistic factors such as the need for blacks to try harder or to have more motivation."[55] In a 2008 study, when white Americans were asked "whether the government has a special obligation to help improve the living standards of African Americans because of longstanding discrimination, the majority said no, with fewer than one in four saying yes."[56] These statements were strong predictors of punitiveness, which was found to be strongly linked to an emphasis on the individualistic causes of "criminal behavior." Those who deflected away from the structural and material causes of crime and criminalization tended to agree that "people commit crime because they don't care about the rights of others or their responsibilities to society" or because they are lazy. Those who were able to recognize the collective, structural, material processes that criminalize race tended to agree that "crime" results from the fact that "our society does not guarantee that everyone has regular employment" or that "poverty and low income are responsible for much of crime."[57]

Studies on race and punitiveness showed that notions of responsibility that individualize harm and deny its collective, material conditions were deeply linked to the racialization of guilt and innocence. White people were likely to attribute their non-criminalized behavior with their own individual moral standing, rather than understanding the role that US laws and institutions have played in protecting white property, wealth, and self-image. White people's investment in their innocence and moral standing relative to non-white people—and their notion that this innocence derives from their own individual choices and achievements—racializes the lack of moral standing at the same time that it criminalizes race. The echoes of psychological studies of guilt and shame that show white tendencies to preserve positive racial self-concept by "let others know" they are in the wrong reverberate strongly here.

CIVIC INNOCENCE AND WHITE RESPONSIBILITY

With a full 25 percent of the world's incarcerated population, the racial punitiveness of the US should not be controversial. The links between carceral punishment and slavery, the convict leasing system (which abolished slavery except for those "duly convicted of a crime," as stated in the Thirteenth Amendment), Jim Crow, the drug wars, policing, and punitive social assistance policies, and their relationship to superexploitation and civic death, are well-documented. The punitiveness that suffuses and structures American life is not a conspiracy, or especially abstract, but, as James Forman, Jr. has put it, the result of "a series of small decisions, made over time, by a disparate group of actors"—legislators, lobby groups, politicians, community groups, individuals. These "small decisions" that institutionalized and racialized punishment contributed to a context determined both by the legacy of slavery and a "politics of responsibility" that has its origins in the nineteenth century, but was concentrated and further consolidated in the 20th. The politics of responsibility is a theory of individualism and "personal discipline" brought into contemporary policy by a generation of white lawmakers, voters, and politicians whose class status had been improved by the G.I. Bill, the New Deal, and federal loan, benefit, and work programs. In addition to receiving these forms of government support, these "lucky few"[58] also benefited from companies that "expanded workforces, built pensions, and distributed stock—a combination that produced the financially luckiest generation of the twentieth century."[59] Thanks to government-sponsored upward mobility, this group had more economic and political influence than prior generations, but tended to view their successes in life as their own achievements rather than thinking in terms of the social, racial, and economic context that made their success possible.[60] Nearly nine out of ten of these "lucky few" were white and born in the US. Among them were the lawmakers and politicians who made and enacted the punitive social policies that catalyzed mass incarceration as the latest phase in a history of racial exclusion, elimination, and hyperexploitation. In this sense, white ignorance was instrumental in the development of mass incarceration.

The faulty individualism of the "politics of responsibility" of Carlson's "lucky few" establishes a dichotomy between those who are worthy and morally upright, and those others who are seemingly unable to be responsible, and are therefore punishable for that unchangeable moral failing. The white sensibilities and moral and affective dispositions that were deemed "civilized" and "civilizable" in the nineteenth century continued to be markers of civic worthiness and participation in the twentieth century and into the twenty-first—implying that those lacking that worthiness are not entitled to enjoy participation in white society on account of these moral failings.

The literal economics of this moral and affective economy cannot be underestimated. This raced notion of personal responsibility and moral worth was instrumental in creating the landscape of racial inequality we see today, with regular white people bearing vastly disproportionate access to capital, property, and investments than non-white people. Behind discourses of "independence" and individualism, these forms of capital—property, investments, financial holdings—are extractive and parasitic on the lives of non-white people.[61] Banks and insurance companies profit from poor and racialized people through credit, interest and mortgage rates; government benefits programs are racialized and criminalized in such a way as to actively inhibit economic security; and the retirement and benefits programs more broadly accessible to white people move capital into the hands of corrections, biochemical, surveillance and security, and tech companies that poison, gentrify, and incarcerate non-white people in the US and abroad.[62]

Under racial capitalism, racialized affect circulates in conjunction with the flows and appropriations of capital, manifesting not just in the personal feelings of individuals, but in the ways that emotional responses become associated with specific kinds of bodies. Guilt and shame circulate in this way, with opportunities to express the associated emotions of fear, threat, resentment, and retrenchment of group identity through the judicial system. As legal scholar Joel Feinberg writes, the essence of legal punishment is the symbolic expression of moral condemnation by the community.[63] Criminal punishment, on this view, is primarily motivated by societal resentment. According to the expressionist position that Feinberg espouses, we are entitled to feelings of hate and vindictiveness toward "criminals" on moral grounds; the function of criminal justice policies is merely to guarantee that that expression happens in a "regular, public legal way."[64] In US law, the courts take it to be true that all criminal statutes are punitive—that is, punishment is what *makes* something a crime. Echoing the eugenicist tones described by Schuller, on Feinberg's view, punishment is an expression of condemnation necessary for the "healthy" functioning of society. Society's innocence, and the innocence of its more powerful members, is maintained by isolating those who are the source of negative affect and resentment. That innocence is justified by using essentializing and individualizing notions of responsibility and blame, so that US society can "protect itself from the troubling recognition" of its own basis in racism.

Rather than an aberration, racialized hyperpunishment and its deflection of blame are a "necessary failure" built into liberal theories of the state. To be innocent is to be a legitimate political agent, in contradistinction to those who are guilty, and therefore symbolically excluded from political participation. For political theorist Andrew Dilts, social contract liberalism and civic republicanism work together to produce "a theory of the criminal subject as irredeemable and therefore unfit for political membership."[65] Dilts names this perspective "liberal republicanism," which has its basis in "the importance of *individual* virtue and moral character as the basis of a strong moral economy and stable polity" (emphasis in the original).[66] Instead of focusing on how excessive forms of criminal punishment in the United States are applied to particular racial groups in violation of liberal norms of equality, what we should be asking, according to Dilts, is, how does excessive punishment "help produce and manage the unstable and changing conception of this particular group?"[67] That is, how do patterns of punishment and the concepts of responsibility attached to them *contribute to* racialization? Dilts's work shows that the production of the felon through patterns of punitive civic exclusion "directly serves the interests of maintaining white supremacist notions of citizenship and does so through the application of a civic disability to some persons, deemed to be [morally] impaired, in order to mark those political members whose standing is beyond question, beyond reproach, and ultimately stable in their whiteness, their innocence, and their normality."[68]

CAUSALITY AND INTENTION IN THE PUNISHMENT PARADIGM

The lengths to which punitive societies like the US go in order to exclude those who are deemed morally unfit to discipline themselves indicate a collective anxiety for self-acquittal. On these stringent racial and moral standards for belonging, white individuals and racializing institutions have innocence to prove. The deflection techniques and urgent performances of white ignorance used by individuals in order to restore innocence are also at work in criminal justice institutions, which use stringent notions of racial intent and causality in order to expand racialized punishment, while retracting responsibility for racial harm.

Criminal justice institutions and employees benefit from a set of laws, norms, and practices that Naomi Murakawa and Katharine Beckett have called "the penology of racial innocence." The penology of racial innocence is a framework that explains the increasing criminalization of racialized individuals, concurrent with the presumption that "criminal justice is innocent of racial power until proven otherwise."[69] As the law has increasingly erased the overt role of race in the study and practice of punishment, the outcome has been *increased* criminal guilt for those who have contact with the criminal punishment system, and *decreased* criminal guilt for those accused of racial discrimination. The criminal justice system, in other words, functions to protect its own innocence at the expense of those who are criminalized and racialized.

The "penology of racial innocence" reveals that guilt and innocence have been shaped by two divergent tendencies: the contraction of the definition of guilt in anti-discrimination law, and the simultaneous expansion of the definition of crime. The expansion of criminal guilt, and the contraction of guilt for racist discrimination, are both enabled by a focus on "racial intent" and "racial causation." As Murakawa and Beckett show, anti-discrimination law is built in such a way as to preserve the innocence of the party accused of discrimination by enforcing a stringent definition of "racial intent."[70] Only "intentional" discrimination is prohibited by the Equal Protection Clause of the Fourteenth Amendment, and "discriminatory purpose" implies "more than awareness of consequences; it implies decision-making for the purpose of discrimination."[71] The legal emphasis on "intention to act according to racial bias" has been a "significant barrier" to changing criminal justice practices that punish differentially according to race, through and beyond incarceration. The focus on intention obscures the role of both systemic factors that may motivate racial discrimination, and of individuals' racial bias, which may not be self-aware or strictly "intentional." Simultaneous to this, an expansion of "discretionary power" for those who work in the criminal justice system, and for the system itself, render intent in parole and sentencing decisions "largely unassailable" and "largely inscrutable."[72] The criminal justice system and its employees, in other words, are completely *unaccountable*, since discriminatory intent is impossible to prove, while those accused of crimes are hyper-guilty, racialized, incontrovertibly identified with a criminal act for which punishment must be administered by the state. This is an institutional manifestation of white ignorance that denies complicity in racism while using the terrain of race in order to establish its own innocent moral standing. As a result, structural racism is reproduced by concepts of responsibility that criminalize race while absolving racializing institutions and the individuals that carry out their goals.

In addition to a stringent standard of "intention," racialized punishment in the US relies on an equally stringent standard of "racial causation" that ensures white innocence and non-white punishability. As Murakawa and Beckett write, "as antidiscrimination law has developed to demand the disaggregation of decision-making points in order to identify 'biased' actions occurring in a single moment, definitions of crime, criminal justice institutions, and discretionary authority have expanded, producing complex causal webs of racial inequality that compound over longer time horizons."[73] A model of accountability whereby racial discrimination occurs in a single moment, through a single intended act, sustains racial innocence—both of the criminal justice system itself, and of those individuals who engage in discriminatory or racist behaviors. If the intent and causation cannot be proven, then innocence is preserved, and no accountability is necessary. This contraction of the definition of responsibility obscures the racial motivations behind punitive policies and practices, creating a precedent for social behavior that serves to preserve that innocence. Notions of accountability that place a strong emphasis on restrictive notions of "racial intent" and "racial causality" contribute to a penology of racial innocence where those who are racialized are hyper-blamed, hyper-punished, excluded and morally condemned on account of their individual failures, whereas white people are deemed morally fit and therefore exempt from active responsibility for racial harm.

We desperately need a framework of responsibility that can bring us beyond our punishment paradigm's fixation on innocence, self-conscious intention, and strictly defined causal contribution. If guilt and shame are implicated in raced, affective economies that determine belonging and rejection in political and moral community, then we need a modality of anti-racist responsibility that accepts the complicity of our very moral frameworks in the project of white supremacy. Without looking at the way affect is involved in reproducing that benefit, white people will be hard pressed to change their behavior and collective habits. Guilt, innocence, shame, and responsibility are not neutral, but are implicated in interpersonal, institutional, and state processes of racialization. As we have seen in this chapter, our notions of civic belonging and moral worthiness are bound up with the institutionalization and normalization of white denial and deflection that ensures white racial innocence.

However, even if they are not effective in prompting changes in behavior or motivating the transformation of material circumstances, shaming and guilt-inducing responses to the collective harm of structural racism are nonetheless intuitive because of the punitive landscape in which we live. The punishment paradigm is predicated on binary, racialized distinctions between good and bad, innocence and guilt, absolution and blame. This is why paradigms of white anti-racist responsibility need to move beyond these binary modalities to take racial complicity, rather than racial innocence, into account as a given. Traditional notions of responsibility in nation-building, morality, and the law tend to focus on whether individuals personally caused or intended harm, and use those concepts to establish or deflect guilt and mete out punishment. This chapter has shown that guilt/innocence binaries are not only inappropriate for collective harms that individuals didn't necessarily cause or intend; they are also counterproductive in anti-racist work insofar as they motivate deflection, distancing, denial, and disavowal in order to preserve moral standing. As long as we are living under racial capitalism, however, white people's responsibility will be complicit. White responsibility for racism can only begin from that place of complicity, or else it will deepen the white ignorance that perpetuates structural racism.

NOTES

1. Steele, "'White Guilt' and the End of the Civil Rights Era," NPR.org, 2006, https://www.npr.org/templates/story/story.php?storyId=5385701.

2. *Indigenous Action Media*, "Accomplices Not Allies: Abolishing the Ally Industrial Complex," *Indigenous Action Media* (blog), May 4, 2014, https://www.indigenousaction.org/accomplices-not-allies-abolishing-the-ally-industrial-complex/.

3. Shelby Steele, *White Guilt: How Blacks and Whites Together Destroyed the Promise of the Civil Rights Era* (HarperCollins, 2009).

4. Indigenous Action Media, "Accomplices Not Allies."

5. Ruth Frankenberg, *White Women, Race Matters: The Social Construction of Whiteness* (Minneapolis: University of Minnesota Press, 1993).

6. Corinne E. Galgay, "Affective Costs of Whiteness: Examining the Role of White Guilt and White Shame" (New York, Columbia University, 2018).

7. Paula Ioanide, *The Emotional Politics of Racism: How Feelings Trump Facts in an Era of Colorblindness* (Stanford University Press, 2015), 1.

8. Ibid., 2.

9. Toni Morrison, *Playing in the Dark* (Knopf Doubleday Publishing Group, 2007), 64–65.

10. Galgay, "Affective Costs of Whiteness: Examining the Role of White Guilt and White Shame," 3.

11. Ibid.

12. Linda Martín Alcoff, *The Future of Whiteness* (John Wiley & Sons, 2015), 146.

13. Helen Block Lewis, *Shame and Guilt in Neurosis* (International Universities Press, 1971).

14. Bernard Williams, *Shame and Necessity* (University of California Press, 2008).

15. Raffaele Rodogno, "Shame and Guilt in Restorative Justice," *Psychology, Public Policy, and Law* 14, no. 2 (2008): 142–76.

16. Ibid.

17. Danielle Sered, *Until We Reckon: Violence, Mass Incarceration, and a Road to Repair* (The New Press, 2019).

18. Brene Brown, "Shame and Accountability," Unlocking Us, 2020.

19. Ibid.

20. June Price Tangney and Ronda L. Dearing, *Shame and Guilt* (Guilford Press, 2003).

21. Lisa B. Spanierman and Mary J. Heppner, "Psychosocial Costs of Racism to Whites Scale (PCRW): Construction and Initial Validation," *Journal of Counseling Psychology* 51, no. 2 (2004): 249–62.

22. Lisa B. Spanierman et al., "White University Students' Responses to Societal Racism: A Qualitative Investigation," *The Counseling Psychologist* 36, no. 6 (August

1, 2008): 839–70, https://doi.org/10.1177/0011000006295589; Galgay, "Affective Costs of Whiteness: Examining the Role of White Guilt and White Shame."

23. Paul Kivel, *Uprooting Racism: How White People Can Work for Racial Justice* (Philadelphia: New Society Publishers, 1996); Nathan R. Todd and Elizabeth M. Abrams, "White Dialectics: A New Framework for Theory, Research, and Practice With White Students 1Ψ7," 2011, https://doi.org/10.1177/0011000010377665; Galgay, "Affective Costs of Whiteness: Examining the Role of White Guilt and White Shame."

24. Rodogno, "Shame and Guilt in Restorative Justice," 156.

25. Charles V. Hamilton and Kwame Ture, *Black Power: Politics of Liberation in America* (Knopf Doubleday Publishing Group, 2011), xvii.

26. Rodogno, "Shame and Guilt in Restorative Justice," 167.

27. Galgay, "Affective Costs of Whiteness: Examining the Role of White Guilt and White Shame."

28. McIntosh, in Galgay.

29. June Price Tangney, Jeff Stuewig, and Debra J. Mashek, "Moral Emotions and Moral Behavior," *Annual Review of Psychology* 58 (2007): 345–72, https://doi.org/10.1146/annurev.psych.56.091103.070145.

30. Rodogno, "Shame and Guilt in Restorative Justice."

31. David M. Amodio, Patricia G. Devine, and Eddie Harmon-Jones, "A Dynamic Model of Guilt: Implications for Motivation and Self-Regulation in the Context of Prejudice," *Psychological Science* 18, no. 6 (June 2007): 524–30, 524.

32. Janet Swim and Deborah Miller, "White Guilt: Its Antecedents and Consequences for Attitudes Toward Affirmative Action," *Personality and Social Psychology Bulletin* 25 (April 1, 1999): 500–514.

33. Jessica Tracy and Richard Robins, "Appraisal Antecedents of Shame and Guilt: Support for a Theoretical Model," *Personality & Social Psychology Bulletin* 32 (October 1, 2006): 1339–51, https://doi.org/10.1177/0146167206290212.

34. Lisa Legault, Jennifer Gutsell, and Michael Inzlicht, "Ironic Effects of Antiprejudice Messages: How Motivational Interventions Can Reduce (but Also Increase) Prejudice," *Psychological Science* 22 (November 28, 2011): 1472–77, https://doi.org/10.1177/0956797611427918.

35. Galgay, "Affective Costs of Whiteness: Examining the Role of White Guilt and White Shame," 100.

36. Shannon Sullivan, *Good White People: The Problem with Middle-Class White Anti-Racism* (SUNY Press, 2014).

37. Sullivan (2014) has argued that white deflection bears a racializing structure, where claiming white middle class innocence at the expense of poor and working class whites reproduces the logic of racial othering through class.

38. Miriyam Aouragh, "'White Privilege' and Shortcuts to Anti-Racism," *Race & Class* 61, no. 2 (October 1, 2019): 3–26, https://doi.org/10.1177/0306396819874629.

39. Mujahid Farid and Laura Whitehorn, "Release Aging People in Prison (RAPP): Challenging the Punishment Paradigm," *Socialism and Democracy* 28, no. 3 (September 2, 2014): 199–202, https://doi.org/10.1080/08854300.2014.957590.

40. Here I mean colonization internal to the US, not the colonization of the mind or consciousness.

41. Kyla Schuller, *The Biopolitics of Feeling: Race, Sex, and Science in the Nineteenth Century* (Duke University Press, 2017), 36.

42. Ibid., 37.

43. Ibid.

44. Damon Young, "The Term 'White Tears' Is Funny, but What It Often Leads to Isn't," The Root, accessed July 14, 2021, https://www.theroot.com/the-term-white-tears-is-funny-but-what-it-often-lead-1790861731.

45. Mamta Motwani Accapadi, "When White Women Cry: How White Women's Tears Oppress Women of Color," *College Student Affairs Journal* 26, no. 2 (2007): 208–15.

46. See "In Defense of Guilt," in Sandra Lee Bartky, *Sympathy and Solidarity: And Other Essays* (Rowman & Littlefield, 2002).

47.Jackie Wang, "Against Innocence," *LIES Feminist Journal* 1, no. 1 (2016), https://www.liesjournal.net/volume1-10-againstinnocence.html.

48.Nazgol Ghandnoosh, "Race and Punishment: Racial Perceptions of Crime and Support for Punitive Policies" (Sentencing Project), accessed July 14, 2021, https://www.sentencingproject.org/publications/race-and-punishment-racial-perceptions-of-crime-and-support-for-punitive-policies/.

49. Ibid.

50. Ibid.

51. Ibid.

52. Ibid.

53. Ghandnoosh, "Race and Punishment," 27.

54. Ibid., 30.

55. Lawrence Bobo et al., "The Real Record on Racial Attitudes," in *Social Trends in American Life: Findings from the General Social Survey since 1972*, ed. Peter V. Marsden (Princeton, NJ: Princeton University Press, 2012).

56. Ghandnoosh, 31.

57. Ibid.

58. Elwood Carlson, *The Lucky Few: Between the Greatest Generation and the Baby Boom* (Springer Science & Business Media, 2008).

59. Evan Osnos, "Can Biden's Center Hold?," *The New Yorker*, n.d.

60. Ibid.

61. Halah Touryalai, "How Banks Are Getting Richer Off The Poor," Forbes, accessed June 7, 2021, https://www.forbes.com/sites/halahtouryalai/2012/04/26/how-banks-are-getting-richer-off-the-poor/.

62. Keeanga-Yamahtta Taylor, *Race for Profit: How Banks and the Real Estate Industry Undermined Black Homeownership* (UNC Press Books, 2019); Ian Haney Lopez, *White by Law: The Legal Construction of Race* (NYU Press, 1996).

63. Many theorists discuss punishment as having utilitarian value ("deterrence"), retributive or "reformative" value, which are often taken for granted in justifying current criminal justice policies. Feinberg, however, rejects these as constituting the

nature and justification of punishment to show that what is most distinctive about criminal punishment is its symbolic, morally expressive value.

64. Igor Primoratz, "Punishment as Language," *Philosophy* 64, no. 248 (1989): 187–205, 603.

65. Andrew Dilts, *Punishment and Inclusion: Race, Membership, and the Limits of American Liberalism* (Fordham University Press, 2014), 14.

66. Ibid.

67. Ibid., 17.

68. Ibid., 194.

69. Naomi Murakawa and Katherine Beckett, "The Penology of Racial Innocence: The Erasure of Racism in the Study and Practice of Punishment," *Law & Society Review* 44, no. 3–4 (2010): 695–730, 695.

70. Ibid., 696.

71. Ibid., 702.

72. Ibid., 696.

73. Ibid., 697.

Chapter 4

Complicit Responsibility and Transformative Whiteness

White fear of failure, anxiety to "get white anti-racism right," and their accompanying forms of paralysis and narcissism are not always laudable, but they are certainly understandable, if not inevitable. The risk of mistakes, miscalculations, and counterproductive interventions is high (if not guaranteed)—especially since deflection, denial, moral purity, urgency, and perfectionism are among the characteristics of some have called "white supremacy culture."[1] Well-intentioned white anti-racists who lose track of their motivation to protect their goodness (and even those who don't) risk being privately corrected or publicly called out in progressive spaces; those attempting to engage in anti-racist education in white-majority spaces must be prepared to face hostility, resentment, resistance, and whitelash—as we have seen with the current movement against critical race theory and armed attacks on Black Lives Matter protesters. White progressives, non-profit workers, activists, and academics fear being accused of racism, even in *–especially* in—their attempts to engage in anti-racist work. Not only is there no one way to get it right, there are endless ways to get it wrong, and white frustration, aggrievement, rage, fear, and beleaguerment in anti-racist work can manifest as racism, even (and sometimes especially) when they are expressed by anti-racist white people trying to be "the best" at destroying white supremacy. There is no way for any individual to transcend whiteness and the harms of white supremacy on their own; there is no action or statement that will, in the short term, restore racial innocence for white people or effectively dissolve the societal harms that cause white people to feel guilt, shame, resentment, and other negative affects having to do with race. But what if the ambiguities of white complicity weren't a fatalistic, deterministic assessment of whiteness, but a place of possibility?

Whiteness is a flexible political position connected to histories of imperialism and colonization that expresses itself through culture, epistemology, ideology, affect, identity, and morality. The chapters of this book have shown that white supremacy permeates our realities, structuring our ways of being, feeling, and knowing. But does this mean that whiteness, and the people it describes, must resign themselves to white supremacy? If white attempts at anti-racism are doomed to reproduce white supremacist dynamics, this would seem to imply that white people either need to un-become white, or that they should passively await instruction from non-white people rather than take initiatives that might risk failure or embarrassment. As Linda Alcoff has so lucidly shown, these two approaches are their own kind of white denial, insofar as they seek to eliminate whiteness, a category that still has meaning and explanatory power, and that may continue to even after the hypothetical death of white supremacy. In place of white disavowal or the abdication of white moral agency, this chapter outlines a framework of responsibility that sees whiteness and white ignorance as supported by active, collective habits and practices that can be changed. As I hope I have shown, whiteness and white dominance have been shaped by different material conditions and the contingent human movements, institutions, and forms of organization that took place in relation to them. As our material conditions change, spurring new social movements and forms of organization, whiteness will change too. It is up to us to take up the possibilities of these changing circumstances. In order to do so, however, white people will need frameworks of responsibility that can move them beyond guilt, shame, and fear—beyond a punishment paradigm so closely tied to the maintenance of white innocence. For this reason, we need a framework of responsibility for white ignorance that acknowledges and works from ambiguity and the possibility of failure, and that attempts to mitigate the white desire to be untarnished and supreme, even in its anti-racism, while still maintaining the rationale and motivation to work against white supremacy. This chapter offers a philosophical approach of this sort: complicit responsibility.

Complicit responsibility deemphasizes guilt, innocence, intention, and causality—*liability*—in favor of a model that focuses on white benefit from, contribution to, and participation in, white supremacy. Where punitive moral frameworks centered on absolution are historically and conceptually individualist, complicit responsibility prioritizes relationality, social position, accountability, and collective action. Traditional notions of responsibility for harm in morality and the law—even when that harm is collective—tend to focus on whether individuals caused and intended harm, and use those concepts to establish or deflect guilt and mete out punishment. But, as psychologists have shown us, guilt/innocence binaries are not only inappropriate for collective harms that individuals didn't themselves cause or intend; they are also counterproductive in anti-racist work because of the disavowal and denial they motivate. These liability-based models of responsibility actively inhibit accountability. As we saw at the end of chapter 3, they render whiteness *unaccountable*, all while hyper-criminalizing, exploiting, and excluding non-whiteness. Liability models also feature and center the moral status of white knowers and actors, creating discourses, policies, and laws that multiply exponentially the question of white individuals' guilt or innocence while deflecting away from material conditions. If the harm in question is white ignorance—the maintenance of white dominance through raced epistemologies of denial and avoidance—then the liability model will reproduce that harm. As white people assume the self-orientation of white liability, deliberating, arguing, blaming and shaming themselves and one another, racism continues to harm BIPOC unabated.

It thus seems important, under such circumstances, for white people to accept, and not disavow, a morally compromised identity one has not chosen. White identity is morally compromised as long as our circumstances are governed by white supremacy and white normativity. Complicit responsibility requires, as scholar Mark B. Brown has put it, "accepting that serious efforts to end white supremacy inevitably lead to mistakes, misunderstandings, and counterproductive outcomes"—but that those serious efforts are necessary and worthwhile for everyone.[2] Only through "robust," but imperfect engagement in struggles for racial justice, can that "tragic" or "complicit" identity can be politicized to transformative effect. But as transformative justice practitioners have shown, people who engage in harm, as white people do, can only transform and be transformed by centering that process on the healing of those who have been harmed: non-white people.

Because white ignorance and white supremacy are normative forces, that centering of the interests of those harmed by racism will be active, rather than passive; responsive, rather than reactive; and will operate both on a "personal" and "institutional" or political register. As political scientist Courtenay Daum writes, white anti-racists must "interrogate the interlocking web of institutional, cultural, and individual practices that work to sustain white power in the US" while distinguishing between "the institutions of white supremacy, which include government and economic institutions, and institutionalized white supremacy"—two mutually supporting registers.[3] Institutionalized white supremacy represents the socio-cultural norms and patterns that uphold white supremacy at the institutional level, and are the precursors to institutional change. In other words, white people can and should take to the streets, demanding that the police be abolished. But, as Daum writes, absent a larger-scale redistribution of power and resources "white people will continue to benefit from institutionalized white supremacy and its associated racial hierarchies."[4] Pursuing only institutional or structural changes without addressing the power that regular white people wield in the everyday lives "allows white power to remain uncontested."[5] A theory of responsibility for white ignorance and complicity must take those endogenous roles in the system into account, and must use those roles to change whiteness and the world in which it dominates. Rather than focusing on being an "exceptional" white person who has somehow managed to transcend the problem of whiteness along with its negative affects, the complicit responsibility framework recognizes that if ordinary white people uphold white benefit and dominance in their everyday lives, they can also challenge it. And as the material wages of whiteness continue to decline from what they once were, and its moral wages diminish as public acknowledgement increases, defensiveness and complicity may have potential as places to begin the work of challenging white ignorance.

Engaging white defensiveness and complicity is not easy work, and there is no one way to do it—no definitive set of "best practices" that will produce the desired "deliverable" sought after by individuals and institutions, and peddled by the growing "anti-racism industrial complex." But while there is no ideal form or blueprint, we can still establish principles and justifications that can orient our efforts. If "achieving innocence," "self-absolution," and "overcoming whiteness" are principles and goals to register and set aside, what principles and goals should be actively taken up—even if incompletely or imperfectly? The complicit responsibility framework is meant to offer some alternative principles to counter the punishment paradigm, and other expressions and justifications of responsibility that have the tendency to reproduce dynamics of white superiority and vanguardism.

The framework I propose in this chapter is meant to capture the responsibility that white people have for ongoing collective harms both in their political and personal lives, from which they benefit. I outline an approach to responsibility for white ignorance that assumes ongoing participation in racist dynamics, while attempting to mitigate and transform the harm of those dynamics into a different way of being and relating with one another, both "interactionally" and institutionally. In order to capture the ways that white people are collectively accountable for harms they did not personally cause or intend (on any stringent notion of causality or intention), both in terms of understanding the harm perpetrated *and* the justice required in response, this chapter begins by reframing the notions of "complicity" and "responsibility."

Complicity is generally understood as something blameworthy to be disavowed. Most normative accounts of complicity frame it as the obverse of responsibility, thereby assuming that to be responsible is to rid oneself of it. This chapter rethinks both concepts together in order to make the opposite claim: that because of the specific features of collective racial harm, complicity should be included in our notions of responsibility, rather than disavowed by it. Most accounts of complicity use individualistic, liability-based moral frameworks even for collective harm, reproducing the binary distinctions between guilt and innocence, goodness and badness, blame and absolution that we saw in previous chapters. As Barbara Applebaum writes, we need a theory of responsibility that "captures the type of complicity that involves participation in wrongs that are normalized as morally good" but that reproduce white ignorance and white domination precisely in their striving for goodness. The chapter begins by looking at the limitations of understanding complicity as in opposition to responsibility. I look at a range of contemporary philosophical accounts of complicity in order to show that separating complicity from responsibility creates barriers for justifying accountability when it comes to normalized, unintended, pre-conscious, uncoordinated forms of harm. I then make the case for the "complicit responsibility model," outlining some of its features. I argue that we need complicit responsibility in order to engage in the process of "transformative whiteness." While liability-based, retributive frameworks motivate disavowal and the seeking of absolution, complicit responsibility understands itself to be risking or effecting the performative reproduction of whiteness in its very attempts to undo it. When white people resist the urge to disavow whiteness, then they can participate in the struggle to desupremacize and transform it from within.

THE LIMITS OF MAINSTREAM THEORIES OF COMPLICITY

Complicity refers to the moral, legal, or political status of individuals or groups as being considered responsible in some way for actions or circumstances for which they are not directly responsible for having caused, and which they did not necessarily explicitly intend.[6] Precisely because "traditional" or mainstream accounts of responsibility in morality and the law tend to focus heavily on causality and intent, accounts of complicity have as well, and have therefore wrestled with the question of how to establish moral agency for members of groups who were not all equally "active" contributors to the harm in question, whether and how collectivities can be responsible at all, and whether individuals can be responsible by the "mere fact of their association with others"—that is, by the fact of group belonging.[7] The literature on theories of complicity is rich, and includes Karl Jaspers's theory of complicity as a metaphysical and existential human condition, Christopher Kutz's groundbreaking theory of "participatory intention" and John Gardner's causal notion of "making a difference to the difference the principal makes." As Timothy McCarty writes, an individual may become complicit through

> through participation in a larger scheme of action such as a criminal conspiracy; they may have been a bystander to a violent crime; they may have participated

> materially in injustice by doing business with a criminal enterprise; they may be members of an organized (or disorganized) collective that perpetuated an injustice; they may simply be citizens of a democratic state; they may unwittingly contribute in some material way to the unjust actions of another, or they may be forced to do so.[8]

The aptness of each of these for capturing something like white ignorance is uneven, because none captures the "twilight state" of white denial that "needs not to know." The reason structural harms like white ignorance require their own special frameworks of complicity and responsibility is because they are social-cultural norms, embodied in laws, institutions, and collective behaviors. The scope of these harms, as we have seen, is vast and multi-dimensional. And while it doesn't make sense to treat all white people as "bystanders to a violent crime" (unless they truly were), it also dilutes and re-normalizes the harm to understand whiteness as the kind of complicity that characterizes all citizens of democratic states, or as simply a natural or metaphysical state of human collective existence. We need a notion of complicity that recognizes the gravity of participating in racial harm, as well as the widespread, often semi-or pre-conscious nature of white participation.

One of the limitations of mainstream accounts of complicity is the assumption that when a wrong has been committed, there will be a clear difference between "principals," whose actions have a *direct* causal effect in producing the wrong, and "accomplices," whose actions may have an *indirect* effect or make a less direct contribution. One could, perhaps, frame white ignorance as a case involving a vast collectivity of "accomplices" where there are no identifiable principals. But even making the distinction maintains the debate around whose harm was "greater" or more directly tied to harm, when in fact all white people should be accountable for the work of combatting white supremacy regardless of their degree of causal contribution. (The unhelpfulness of that distinction notwithstanding, the term "accomplice" does have appeal for the complicit work of white anti-racism, as Indigenous Action Media have written.)

In keeping with the dominance of utilitarian, consequentialist, and virtue-based accounts in mainstream philosophy, accounts of complicity tend to vacillate between intention, causality, and the cultivation of good character, usually rejecting a focus on one in favor of a focus on the other.[9] This makes them inadequate for cases where narrow definitions of intention and causality are used as deflectionary tactics, as we saw in chapter 3's discussion of the penology of racial innocence. Many accounts also tend to face a temporal problem, insofar as they blur or neglect the distinction between descriptive and normative complicity—between being answerable for having contributed to harm in the past tense, and future-oriented accountability to others for repair. For this reason, many accounts struggle to describe unintentional, pre-conscious, normalized participation in the harm of structural racism, and are hard pressed to justify a normative response. In many cases, when attempting to avoid retributive focus on causality and intention, normative responses fall back on psychologizations of collective harm that cannot get past changing the attitudes and characters of individual participants. The consequence is that these accounts are ill-suited to address the structural ignorance at work in unstructured, disorganized, group-based forms of harm that individuals don't necessarily cause, intend, or control, and of which they are not straightforwardly cognizant.[10]

In the United States, the legal basis for conferring the roles of principal and accomplice—a way of attributing liability for involvement in a crime or wrong—is the degree of causal contribution. This sets the stage for denials of complicity and responsibility like those we have seen in the "debates" around critical race theory, which prohibit making individuals in the present responsible for the past actions of members of their own identity group. As the liberal story goes, if I never use racial slurs and didn't personally own other human beings, I did not cause racial harm, and cannot be made responsible for it.

Legal philosopher John Gardner's account of responsibility is an example of this focus on the causal contribution of individuals. Gardner argues that complicity arises when someone who is not a "principal" wrongdoer "makes a difference to the difference that the principal makes."[11] On this view, a complicit person should be thought of as an accomplice to the wrong who can be shown to be part of the causal chain of events. The difference between principals and accomplices, or complicit agents, is where one is situated on the causal chain leading up to the wrong or harm. The explicit aim of this approach is to reject the notion that one can be a complicit participant in moral wrongs caused by others *without* any causal effect: if we don't reject non-causal accounts, there will be no moral basis for avoiding its "moral taint."[12] This account of complicity takes causal contribution to be synonymous with moral taint, on the assumption that responsibility for harm will conversely involve the *absence* of moral taint. This definition encourages quibbling about the degree of causation, and remains stuck in a moral paradigm that aims to ensure the moral purity of those who cannot be proven to have made a causal contribution. In this way, accounts that focus on causal contribution import white ignorance's anxiety to maintain innocence as the crux of moral responsiveness.

Accounts that focus on intention over causality also encounter this problem. On Christopher Kutz's important account of "complicitous accountability," for example, complicity is captured by the notion of "participatory intention"[13]—a notion that accepts that the causality standard fails to capture the moral responsibility of participants whose individual contributions may not make a significant difference. For Kutz, if individuals are "only responsible for the effects they produce, then the result of this disparity between collective harm and individual effect is the disappearance of individual accountability."[14]

Kutz's account is groundbreaking insofar as it considers collective accountability to "rely on an underlying theory of complicity."[15] His "Complicity Principle" is meant to account for the ways that individuals are necessarily involved in collective realities and relationships that simultaneously implicate them in harm, and have the power to "make a community." This framing is an important contribution to conversations on collective forms of harm. But Kutz's account has difficulty accounting for "unstructured harms" like participation in white supremacy or capitalism. His promising notion of "complicitous accountability" relies on participants having a "common conception" of their actions,[16] which is not the case for the common participation of white people with a range of ideological commitments, goals, and class identities in white benefit. For this reason, Kutz states explicitly that his Complicity Principle doesn't obtain for "aggregate, marginal individual contributions" like participation in capitalism or environmental degradation. Even if his definition of intention is meant to be loose enough to capture many kinds of participation in harm, it still relies on individuals' conscious, concerted choices, and the affective responses that accompany them.

Legal philosophers Chiara Lepora and Robert Goodin have attempted to get around the "platitudes about the role of intention" by focusing on the etymological root of complicity as "acting with," regardless of shared intent or "common conceptions" of projects that result in harm.[17] They adopt a minimalist notion of complicity as "knowledge without purpose," where all that is morally relevant is "to acknowledge that you are engaging with and indeed contributing to wrongdoing, even if you do so only in order to do more good on balance." This preferable to denying "that you are doing anything wrong at all by contributing to wrongdoing, on the grounds that your intentions are pure."[18] Even though this account attempts to avoid intention-based denial—the defense that one "didn't mean it"—it still individualizes harm and purpose, neglecting the ways that collective racial harms like white ignorance protect group-based interests through normalization and deflection, without necessarily being entirely self-conscious. The notion of "knowledge without purpose" still doesn't capture the contradictory "twilight state" character of white ignorance, or the ways that institutions, laws, norms, morality, and culture conspire to reproduce white benefit.

In these approaches to complicity, we can see that mainstream theory is primarily focused on measuring—and avoiding—a level of individual moral taint linked to causality, intention, purpose, and cognizance. Even philosophical notions of "shared responsibility" like Larry May's, developed to account for participation in genocide, maintain the normative preoccupation with distancing and disavowal in understanding shared responsibility to be an existential, attitudinal exercise of "who one chooses to be."[19] If complicity is responsibility for shared attitudes, then accountability is cultivating the character and disposition to recognize one's harmful ways of knowing, and to feel enough shame to want to "reconcile" that harm in the future.[20] But in linking agency to existential attitudes, May's account of "shared responsibility" excludes those on the receiving end of harm from the accountability process. In this way, as Bailey writes, May's account re-centers white people as moral agents and decision-makers, whose responsibility consists in their vocal dissent or rejection to past attitudes.[21] The focus on attitude, character, and disposition also equates responsibility with *acknowledgement*. As Applebaum warns, May "does explicitly claim that one can relieve oneself of responsibility for the crimes that other people commit if one opposes the wrong or if one dissents."[22] While dissent can be an important response to structural wrongs in which one is complicit, one's social position may make this approach counterproductive by motivating performances of the "right" attitude that are incorrectly thought to redress harm, like performative anti-racist signaling that does little to redistribute material resources or change material conditions.

While each of these accounts clarifies the different ways that one can participate in harm without being its "principal" instigator, each, in its own way, also encourages the dynamics of denial by focusing on individuals' causal contributions, self-transparent shared intentions, cognizance, and correct affective expression. It is true that individuals do contribute causally to the persistence of white ignorance; that they may act "intentionally" to maintain the benefits they derive from whiteness; that they may have some knowledge of structural racism even if they do not intend or have the "purpose" to participate in it. It is also true that attitudinal changes and the individual choices we make are an important part of anti-racism. What I am suggesting here, however, is that with the exception of Kutz's notion of "complicitous accountability," responsibility is understood by mainstream ethics to be *in opposition* to complicity. Accountability and responsibility, on these accounts, become a normative ideal that repudiates the moral taint of complicit action.[23] As we have seen in previous chapters, this kind of moral ideals inhibit accountability for white ignorance, motivating the pursuit of absolution rather than the pursuit of racial justice and the transformation of material circumstances. The remainder of this chapter thus develops the notion of complicit responsibility.

REFRAMING COMPLICITY

Because of the white ignorance of mainstream philosophy and legal theory with respect to racial harm, accounts of complicity—even those like May's that attempt to account for collective harms like genocide—tend to ignore the systems of support for racist wrongs that make white ignorance continuous, rather than acute. The mainstream accounts of complicity we saw above, while illuminating in some ways, ignore the fact that it is precisely that systemic support that implicates group members in harms they didn't cause or intend, and which go beyond their capacity to "choose" their attitudes or "who they want to be." In addition to their perpetrator-group solipsism, many mainstream accounts fall short in their lack of attention to the ways that social and political position impacts responsibility for structural wrongs, applying universal moral notions of responsibility to collective actions committed out of structural ignorance, naive self-interest, or collectively accepted norms. A notion of responsibility that can respond to white ignorance must, then, refer to the position or role actors hold within systems of power, and the ways that that social position implicates actors in harmful individual and collective relationships.[24]

Barbara Applebaum's White Complicity Pedagogy is a much-needed alternative to mainstream frameworks in its finding the basis for responsibility not in causal contribution, self-conscious intent, or "chosen" attitudes, but in the fact of benefit. Applebaum ties "benefitting from" to "contributing to": to be in a position to benefit from a history of white dominance and priority simply *is* to enact and perpetuate racism. While white people are not at fault or to blame for the locations they occupy, they are nonetheless responsible because of the various forms of unjust benefit derived from their whiteness. This has little to do with how one feels or what one believes, what one did or didn't do, or the attitudes one has. In this way, Applebaum's white complicity pedagogy demonstrates the crucial significance of *unintended* participation, pre-or un-conscious knowledge and ignorance, and social position as the bases of complicity and responsibility. The "white complicity claim"

> maintains that white people, through the practices of whiteness and by benefitting from white privilege, contribute to the maintenance of systemic racial injustice. However, the claim also implies responsibility in its assumption that the failure to acknowledge such complicity will thwart whites in their efforts to dismantle unjust racial systems and, more specifically, will contribute to the perpetuation of injustice.[25]

The white complicity claim intervenes in the resistant rhetoric of denial, distancing, and deflection by identifying the recognition of complicity as "a necessary (albeit not sufficient) condition of challenging systemic racial oppression."[26] Given the ways that white innocence is socially, culturally, and politically sanctioned, the white complicity claim does key work in its presumption of the fact that because "racism is often perpetuated through *well-intended* white people, being morally good may not facilitate and may even frustrate the recognition of such responsibility."[27]

White complicity pedagogy gets around the problems posed by more individualistic theories of complicity in collective wrongs, insofar as it recognizes that "if racism involves a system of group privilege that white people benefit from and that simultaneously marginalizes people of color, such systemic privilege is not something that white people can renounce at will."[28] In response to liberal philosophical views that take individuals' capacity for transcendence for granted, theorizing autonomous rational agents as capable of "overcoming any existing contingencies,"[29] Applebaum's notion of complicity has as its basis the view that "one cannot transcend the social system that frames how one makes meaning of oneself and the social world within which one is embedded."[30] This non-transcendence of the complicity claim doesn't imply that the circumstances cannot be transformed; only that transformation cannot occur through the efforts of lone individuals, and that that transformation cannot happen from a position of moral purity and innocence for white people that imagines that whiteness has already been abolished.

Applebaum's white complicity claim can serve both the descriptive and normative aspects of complicit responsibility. In the case of the former, it can overcome claims to white innocence by capturing the ways that white people are collectively accountable for harms they did not personally cause or intend; the ways that they benefit from circumstances that are not under their individual control; and the ways that those circumstances inhibit their recognition of those benefits and their accompanying behaviors. In the case of the normative dimension of complicit responsibility, white complicity pedagogy can support a rationale for engagement in collective, coalitional anti-racist activities by refusing moral purity, innocence, and transcendence, being nonetheless forward-looking, and focusing on the possibilities offered by one's particular social and political positions, relationships, and material circumstances.

Complicit responsibility and Applebaum's White Complicity Pedagogy take their inspiration from Iris Young's Social Connection Model.[31] Following Hannah Arendt's distinction between guilt and responsibility, the Social Connection Model serves to describe a model of responsibility for structural injustice, rather than the "personal," blameworthy wrongs for which individuals are "liable," or guilty.[32] Arendt argued for a strong distinction between guilt and responsibility in response to the question of German guilt, claiming that "where all are guilty, nobody is. Guilt, unlike responsibility, always singles out; it is strictly personal. . . . It is only in a metaphorical sense that we can saw we feel guilty for the sins of our fathers or our people or mankind, in short, for deeds we have not done, although the course of events may well make us pay for them."[33] Guilt, Arendt controversially claimed, "obscures the real issues"—namely, the harms of the Nazi regime. Guilt and responsibility, for Arendt, are thus two separate registers—one moral, one political—which Young develops in her account.[34]

While I don't think that what is moral can be separated from what is political, as chapters 2 and 3 showed, Young is concerned to develop a framework of responsibility that doesn't hold those most affected by structural, historical wrongs to blame for them. This is a direct reaction to the well-established and deeply engrained discourse of "personal responsibility" that erroneously holds individuals responsible for the poverty, sexism, or racism that they endure, while absolving policy makers and members of society who tacitly or passively support those wrongs.[35] To this end, Young distinguishes between two perspectives. The first, the "liability model," refers to wrongs or harms that are personally caused, intentionally or unintentionally, by an individual, and for which that individual can be faulted. An acute act of overt racism, even if unintended, merits attributing fault, an apology, and the making of amends. This, for Young, would merit a liability response. Matters of collective harm involving norms, laws, and institutions, however, involve a different kind of responsibility. These structural wrongs, for Young, are distinct from wrongs that are the result of interpersonal interactions, as well as specific policies or laws, since none of these can adequately represent the "multiple, large scale, and relatively long term" accumulated sources of harms like homelessness, climate dysregulation, sweat shop labor—or white ignorance. Structural injustice, for Young, refers to "harms for which no particular agent" can be singly identified as the wrongdoer.[36]

For systemic, pervasive harms involving multiple interactions, actors, institutions, norms, and laws, Young develops the Social Connection Model. The features of this model are that it is (1) not isolating (it doesn't pin harm or the response to harm on an individual person, considered in isolation), (2) it judges background conditions (rather than finding them politically or morally neutral), (3) it's more forward-looking than backward-looking (motivating actors to take up their agency to change ongoing states of affairs, rather than looking to assess blame for past wrongs), (4) it takes responsibility to be shared (no single person is fully responsible), and (5) it is discharged through collective action. This model can be descriptively and normatively concurrent with the liability model, and it is meant to capture that "all agents who contribute by their actions to the structural processes that produce injustice have responsibilities to work to remedy those injustices."[37] [38] When social processes "put large categories of persons under a systematic threat of domination and deprivation of the means to develop and expand the capacities, at the same time that these processes enable others to dominate or have a wide range of opportunities for developing and expanding their capacities," no single person is to blame, but all who are involved in those processes should have some role in changing them on account of their involvement.[39]

Young does not spell out how the Social Connection Model (SCM) should be carried out beyond describing its features, and offering some "parameters" to assist with that deliberation: when assessing one's role, one should take "power, privilege, interest, and collective ability" into account.[40] In other words, understanding one's social position is an essential part of the process of "discharging" or acting on one's responsibility by virtue of social connection. Where Young gives us less support is in navigating the specific paradoxes of white agency—and particularly the tendency for white anti-racist morality to reproduce white domination. The SCM gives a general approach and an alternative to blame and guilt centered models, but the particular problem of responsibility for white ignorance requires more specificity because of the tendency for white moral agency to be counterproductive, ineffective, or conservative in response to racism. The SCM also doesn't describe how responsibility might be shared across coalitions, and doesn't address the specifics of accountability across the various identities and social positions involved in structural processes. That is why I offer an additional (provisional) framework with its own features, inspired by the SCM, but meant specifically to address the issue of white accountability. Because transformative justice practitioners have some privileged insights into the process of addressing harm non-punitively at the community level, I have incorporated some of those insights into the features of the framework. The framework is meant to capture two registers of complicity: one that expresses the implication and involvement white people have by virtue of the benefit they derive from participating in racial harm, and another that expresses the normative pressure to act in a future-oriented, change-making or supportive way *in response to* that involvement.

THE FEATURES OF COMPLICIT RESPONSIBILITY

Rejects Transcendence

The complicit responsibility model recognizes that no individual can transcend the limitations of whiteness and white moral socialization. Neither can individuals choose to transcend or disavow whiteness itself.[41] Just as whiteness as a relational social position cannot be selectively transcended or purified (which would itself be an expression of white supremacist thinking), neither can the harms caused by white supremacy and white ignorance. These harms are ongoing, and even if they were not, accountability for them would, according to the transformative justice approach, involve healing and not curing, addressing, grieving, and accounting—transforming—instead of denying or deflecting. "Rejecting transcendence" acknowledges that white attempts to respond adequately to racism will necessarily involve the double-bind of whiteness and the political tensions associated with the way the benefits of whiteness circulate through white bodies. "Rejecting transcendence" is a way of acknowledging—and discouraging—the tendency for white people to engage in anti-racism as a means for establishing or restoring moral purity.

Transformative approaches do not seek to absolve and redeem, but to mitigate harm and to end the systems that allowed the harm to take place. This feature of the complicit responsibility model is compatible with prefigurative practices that attempt to enact a better world; but still does not think that the fact of whiteness can be transcended in such spaces. Pre-figurative spaces are precisely those where white people should likely be quite vigilant about, and on account of, their whiteness.

"Rejecting transcendence" also implies that white social connections and communities should not be transcended—especially if those connections and communities are white. This is not an endorsement of segregated spaces. But if our movements want to transform our society, white people need to acknowledge the "mobs" that are "with them," and tend to them, rather than disavowing them. Those of us who are white, are connected to white majority spaces, and have relationships within them, are uniquely positioned to engage in anti-racist work—the nature of which will of course vary depending on the specifics of one's role, skills, power, interest, etc. Contrary to Larry May's account of "shared responsibility," working with these kinds of relationships is an expression of collective white accountability. It is the willingness to address harm in which one participates by facing, and dealing with, the consequences in the communities white people come from. This work can be difficult, and sometimes dangerous, and doesn't often win the credibility and "color capital" of more performative kinds of anti-racism undertaken in non-white spaces, but it is unquestionably worthwhile, and necessary.

Seeks Partial, Multiple Solutions in the Present, Informed by the Past, for a Different Future

This feature of the complicit responsibility model is a modified version of Young's "future-orientation" of the Social Connection Model. It is meant to capture the way that histories of domination, exploitation, migration, and trauma set the stage for where we are today, and reverberate through our habits and ways of being. It is "complicit" in its taking in the complexities and impurities of these historical and geographical legacies and using them as resources for grounding and supporting anti-racist work. Rather than a politics of "equivalence" or "victim bonding," this feature refers to the histories that generate social position, motivating white people to understand their role in changing states of affairs. In this sense, the complicit responsibility model looks backward in order to look forward—but does so in order to learn, not to attribute blame; in order to develop a complex picture of collective white benefit and implication in order to justify a future-oriented response.

This element of the complicit responsibility model is also "complicit" in its recognition that partial, imperfect actions in the present can nonetheless be part of the process of reshaping what is possible. This is not synonymous with "reformism" or the "gradualism" adopted by those who thought slavery should be gradually phased out, but an approach that takes on meaningful immediate change, even if those measures are unlikely to end white supremacy overnight, or in this lifetime. As liberation theologian Sharon Welch writes,

> The extent to which an action is an appropriate response to the needs of others is constituted as much by the possibilities it creates as by its immediate results. Responsible action does not mean one individual resolving the problems of others. It is, rather, participation in communal work, laying the groundwork for the creative response of people in the present and in the future. Responsible action means changing what can be altered in the present even though a problem is not completely resolved. Responsible action provides partial resolutions and the inspiration and conditions for further partial resolutions by others. It is sustained and enabled by participation in a community of resistance."[42]

Centers Those Who Have Been Harmed

According to transformative justice practitioners, even though a transformative justice (TJ) process means to give all participants the resources they need to heal their relationships, and focuses on consequences over punishment, an accountability process still centers the needs and goals of the person who was harmed. While I acknowledge that it is controversial to use the TJ approach to address the problem of white ignorance, since the approach was developed by and for communities marginalized and targeted by the criminal punishment system, I find this insight to be particularly helpful: an accountability process supports the person who engaged in harm in meeting the needs of the person who was harmed. Given what we have seen in the chapters of this book, it is a fact that white people need support, education, and alternative habit-formation in order to de-center and de-supremacize themselves on a collective level—and the most difficult aspects of this work should be undertaken by white people themselves.

This division of labor is important to white accountability, even if non-white people on the receiving end of white ignorance and other expressions of coloniality and white supremacy hold the expertise when it comes to counter-hegemonic epistemologies and strategies of resistance. White ignorance tends to "set aside" the knowledges and perspectives needed for a freer and more liberated world because they run counter to the capitalist and colonial enterprise that upholds the status of whiteness.[43] Accountability for white ignorance on the complicit responsibility model maintains that in a world where racism is the product of colonial, capitalist relations, confronting white ignorance is fundamentally about the safety, self-determination, flourishing, and well-being of non-white people. TJ processes seek support and facilitation for bringing that reality about.

But TJ practitioners are also committed to the flexibility of an accountability process; many maintain that rather than being strictly outcome-based, TJ can be thought of as a personal and collective set of practices that shift our collective responses to harm without relying on the state processes that reproduce harm. Crucially for the purposes of responding to white ignorance, a TJ process does not need to directly involve the person who was harmed, even if their needs and grievances are the impetus for the process. This is to say that white people can, on the complicit responsibility model, engage in the work of responding to collective harm without demanding the energy and participation of people of color. As Mariame Kaba and Shira Hassan write, all parties involved in an accountability process must consent to participating.[44] A major contribution of the complicity model of responsibility is that it provides a basis for collectively taking on the political interests of those whose identities we might not share, without disavowing the identities and positions that are our own.

Aims for Personal, Relational, and Political Change

As TJ practitioner Shannon Perez-Darby writes in "The Secret Joys of Accountability: Self-Accountability as a Building Block for Change," community accountability models "strive to address violence using community-centered responses based outside of the state's criminal legal system."[45] While I do believe there is a place for faulting and blaming white perpetrators of racial violence, we have seen that white ignorance operates in partnership with an institutional punishment paradigm that aims primarily to uphold white innocence for individuals, institutions, and the nation. This means that accountability for white ignorance should take place in such a way as to inhibit its instrumentalization of the criminal punishment system.

Perez-Darby writes that "we need to build the capacity within our movements to respond to violence, and I believe that work begins with building *our own internal capacity* to look at and be responsible for our choices."[46] Perez-Darby is referring to two registers of TJ accountability: community accountability, and self-accountability. Neither of these is guilt or fault based, but each is a dimension of the work required to end the conditions that produce violence. This is consistent with Young's contention that personal responsibility and structural injustice are not mutually exclusive; both can co-exist as intertwined characterizations of harm, and as responses to it.

For all the ways that racism is structural, a social structure, as Young writes, "exists only in the actions and interactions of persons."[47] This means that in order for structures to change, individuals must see their role in perpetuating them, and must address the reproduction of harm on the personal, relational, and communal level. While self-accountability doesn't have an individualistic motive, since it is a building block in changing the circumstances that give rise to violence,[48] it takes into account the fact that individual white people do have the responsibility for taking whiteness into account, for developing the skills and emotional resilience needed to reflect on and modify their behavior, and to work with others in order to support that change. As Perez-Darby writes, "I often hear people ask questions about how they can hold someone else accountable. So often, people jump to an external definition of accountability that is about other people assuming responsibility for their actions rather than imagining accountability as an internal process."[49]

This dynamic is endemic to white anti-racist spaces, where there can be intense jockeying to demonstrate one's own good whiteness relative to the failings and mistakes of others. While I do think that it is important for white people to support one another in being accountable I do not think that guilt, blame, and shame are effective tools for doing so. In order to divest oneself of the methods of the punishment paradigm we saw in chapter 3, relational and collective accountability for white ignorance require deep personal work—of course, with the support of others. Complicit responsibility takes the personal, relational, and communal registers to be interconnected: each involves the others. At each of these registers, complicit responsibility suggests that white people challenge punitive whiteness and create connections with ourselves, our communities, and one another that resist the punishment paradigm, learning from inevitable mistakes along the way.

Role-based

Young characterizes responsibility for justice not as having "directed a process" or "intended its outcomes," but in terms of the ways that roles and positions are practiced and taken up.[50] The role of teacher, for example, entails a set of activities and obligations, and responsibility refers to morally appropriate ways of carrying them out. Positions and roles do change, and they are therefore an important feature of complicit responsibility insofar as they describe one's particular social position as white, a flexible, context-specific category. While all white people are responsible by virtue of their having benefitted from whiteness, whiteness positions people differently in terms of class, ethnicity, occupation, geographical location, gender, sexuality, and relational landscape. Complicit responsibility takes these roles, origins, and social locations into account, especially with regard to forward-looking action, treating these as places in which, and from which, the personal, relational, political, and institutional work of anti-racism can be done.

While the complicit responsibility framework is meant for responsibility to be carried out as an active practice, it is possible that one's social position will determine that the most effective and active contribution one can make is to step aside, support another individual, quietly donate money or time, or amplify the work of others. In this sense, complicit responsibility is anti-white-saviorist, in asking white people to identify and interrogate where and how their specific role and position can make them the most effective. The advantage of this framework is that it sees "contribution" both in the backwards-looking and forward-looking directions: white people contribute to white supremacy through the ways that they benefit, and can now use those positions and locations in order to contribute to the de-supremicization of whiteness through coalitional, context-specific work. The use of one's position as a white person will necessarily be complicit under conditions of capitalist white supremacy.

Involves Resistance and Risk

The complicit responsibility framework takes white anti-racist work to involve both resistance and risk. It involves resistance in two senses: in the first sense, resistance refers to the internal blockages and inhibitions that white people encounter when faced with the need to confront their own whiteness and the deadly effects of whiteness in the world. This first kind of resistance is descriptive. It is internal, collective, and institutional, and includes the resistance that white people have to acknowledge racial benefit, and the resistance institutions have to shifting white normativity.[51] It also includes the white epistemic resistance to complex, creative non-white knowledges and forms of organization, and the powerful role they have had in shaping our world.[52]

Resistance in the second sense is normative and external, and refers to the ways that whiteness can be shifted through collective action. As Sharon Welch writes, making change requires an "ethic of risk" that construes "responsible action as the creation of a matrix of further resistance."[53] That resistance will require taking the risk of facing whiteness' internal resistance. Accounting for the epistemic barriers of whiteness is undertaken at great risk to one's self-conception because it involves "reconceptualizing one's relation not only to one's self but also to one's community and belief systems."[54] Because whiteness cannot be disavowed, the process of taking responsibility for white ignorance reveals the truth of complicity, destabilizing both individual and collective white self-conception—a cognitive state that Linda Alcoff has called "white double consciousness." This destabilization without disavowal can only happen through work within and across racial, cultural, and national communities that will necessarily involve internal and cross-coalitional friction—in both the descriptive and normative sense.[55]

Maintains Complicit Associations

The complicit responsibility model doesn't advocate for increased complicity with white supremacy, but for recognizing its existence while simultaneously working against it. This paradoxical position doesn't use complicity to "opt out," but to "opt in" with respect to the communities and relationships one is a part of.[56]

What this means is breaking with a long history of definitions of complicity that have demands for dissociation and disavowal built into them.[57] While dissociation may be helpful for justifying draft dodging or conscientious objecting, it is less helpful for white ignorance, which is not a set of circumstances from which one can remove oneself.[58] What theories that advocate for dissociation and disavowal imply for those taking responsibility for white ignorance is that one can discharge one's responsibility for white ignorance by distancing oneself from communities, institutions, friendships, and families where white ignorance is endemic. Complicit responsibility makes the opposite claim: while some white people may face threats for their anti-racist activities, when possible, and within reason, white people should continue to associate with white environments where they have organic connections and relationships, or where they can engage in institutional change and political education. This is another way of expressing the fact that white supremacy will not be dismantled by one white person disavowing where they come from.

This is not necessarily to say that white Americans should "Go Home to Your 'Dying' Hometown," as a recent *New York Times* op-ed claimed—even if its author does make a good case.[59] It is to say, rather, that white people should use their social position to resist white ignorance in creative ways from wherever they are. As TJ practitioner and advocate Shira Hassan has said of the beginnings of her work, "building relationships with people who cause harm is the most TJ thing we were doing."[60] This is not to say that white people with other intersecting identities or vulnerabilities should put themselves at significant risk, or that all white people committed to white supremacist ideology can be reformed. Some cannot. There is, however, work for white people to do to resist white ignorance at the collective level that they may be particularly well-placed to do. In this sense, rather than engaging in passive allyship, or only seeking out anti-racist contexts that will allow them to accumulate "color capital," they can use their social positions in order to be active "accomplices." This work—as the term "accomplice" connotes—cannot be done by individuals alone, and cannot be done outside of coalitions.

Accountable coalitions involve committing to our own communities—the ones we are from, or the ones we have come to call our own. As Hamilton and Ture write in "The Myths of Coalition," "One of the most disturbing things about almost all white supporters has been that they are reluctant to go into their own communities—which is where the racism exists—and work to get rid of it."[61] White involvement in effective and supportive coalitions for racial justice should vary depending on "the white person's own class background and environment."[62] Crucially, organizing white people into anti-racism, according to Hamilton and Ture, can and should only be done by other white people, who have access to places and spaces that non-white people do not have. White people, they write, "need 'freedom schools' as badly as the black communities. Anglo-conformity is a dead weight on their necks too. All this is an educative role crying to be performed by those whites so inclined."[63] "The Myths of Coalition" was written in the heat of the Black Power struggle of the late 1960s, and the call for white people to engage other white people's white ignorance remains just as strong today. To engage in that work will not absolve individual white people of their participation in racism. But it can be transformative in contributing to the slow, uncertain process of ending racial harm and the conditions that bring it about.

TRANSFORMING THE CONDITIONS OF WHITE RACIAL HARM: TRANSFORMATIVE WHITENESS

Transformative justice seeks to respond to harm without reproducing more harm, breaking intergenerational cycles of violence and abuse tied to patterns of oppression. Rather than punishing harm through retribution, or restoring the conditions that existed prior to harm, transformative justice is meant to repair and heal relationships and shift harmful dynamics beyond our current ways of being—beyond prisons, beyond intimate partner abuse, beyond the police. Transformative justice addresses not just acute instances of harm, but the conditions that gave rise to them, and understands "shame, blame, revenge, and isolation" as tactics of the state meant to punish difference.[64] This is why the transformative justice approach was created primarily by, and for, those most vulnerable to state violence, and who have been therefore been unable to rely on the state for justice: Indigenous people, Black people, immigrants, people of color, queer, trans and Two-Spirit people. Transformative justice is meant to transform the material conditions of our lives, from our institutions and decision-making procedures down to our interpersonal relationships, because it understands harm to be rooted in systems of oppression. Transforming our society means transforming it for all its participants, radically remaking our relationships toward one another apart from violent systems of punishment, enforcement, and control. I have been suggesting in this chapter that white ignorance demands a transformative framework beyond guilt and liability, and I'll conclude here with a reflection on the necessity of practicing "transformative whiteness."

Transformative justice is a context-specific and community based paradigm committed to working outside punitive state institutions. Without a specific context of harm in which a community accountability process can take place, those who are transformative justice practitioners may be skeptical of its application to white collective harm in general. However, the persistent deadly consequences of white ignorance show us that white approaches to collective harm have not been effective. This concluding meditation on transformative whiteness intends to reorient white responsibility away from punishment and toward something else, while refusing to be an apologist for white normativity, white supremacy, and the harms of white ignorance.

In chapter 3, we saw that guilty affect—that is, feeling, expressing, and projecting self-blame for structural racism—has a paralyzing impact on the agency of those who participate in societal harm. In a racist social context, some of that paralysis is rooted in moral othering, an anxiety to reestablish personal goodness and innocence relative to an abstract or real non-white interlocutor or judge. This anxiety, while in part an earnest desire to act well with respect to others, is also a manifestation of a political and cultural punishment paradigm that responds to harm with retribution, perpetuating fear and resentment as a result. Transformative justice practitioners like Mariame Kaba describe transformative justice processes as "empowering" the person who caused harm to be accountable, rather than disempowering them. While this term is awkward for describing the forms of accountability meant to dismantle white power and superiority, I want to suggest that this should be true of transformative whiteness, too, in the sense that white people should be empowered to take up the fight against white supremacy, settler colonialism, and racial-capitalism—with the proviso that these efforts will necessarily be dialectical, collective, prone to failure, and directly responsive to the needs, demands, and strategies recommended by non-white and colonized people.

Just as transformative justice practitioners recommend, transformative whiteness would require those who participate in harm to develop systems of accountability and support that can help them in the contradictory process of desupremicizing whiteness.

Because the transformative justice approach assumes a long-term process where no parties are disposable, and where accountability is undertaken in community with the goal of transforming behaviors, relationships, and the social forces that undergird them, I consider it to be a promising heuristic for white ignorance. I recognize, however, that there are reasons to be circumspect about it. The first—which I hope will quickly be dispelled here—is that non-punitive approaches to whiteness are tantamount to being "soft" on white complicity, or worse, that they coddle white supremacists. The fine line between supporting accountability and "enabling" the person who caused harm is well documented in the accounts of TJ practitioners,[65] and is likely to arise in effective efforts to be complicitly responsible when white people engage, organize, and educate other white people. That, however, is much less "soft," much more difficult, and much more effective than white liberal or radical-liberal disengagement from those considered to be the "real" racists. The goal of transformative whiteness is for white people to transform themselves and other white people around them, in place of opting for guilt-induced deflection, denial, or quick face-saving solutions at the expense of other white people and people of color, and given the history of whiteness, that work is not likely to be easy. Transformative whiteness is also not synonymous with forgiveness. According to complicit responsibility, questions of forgiveness, blame, and guilt are a distraction from the deeper, longer-term work of shifting the material, institutional and interpersonal dynamics of structural racism.

The police murders of George Floyd and Breonna Taylor prompted many white newcomers to join the movement for community responses to harm, and against punitive, racist institutions like the police. Tens of millions of people were estimated to have taken to the streets in the summer of 2020. Zoom calls on building mutual aid and rapid response networks in place of calling the police, and panels on abolishing the police, attracted hundreds of participants. The public interest in non-violent, non-punitive responses to harm was thrilling, and when Minneapolis announced that it would defund its police department, it seemed that a real paradigm shift might be underway.

But white support—in terms of political involvement and opinion—has waned significantly since that summer, and this is a longstanding pattern. When movements for Black liberation emerge, there "always comes a point when white allies realize the gravity of the movement and want to make sure they are on the right side of history."[66] White participation of this kind, while it does lend visibility, tends to overshadow the courage and demands of the

Black activists who initiated the movement. Citing white participation in the civil rights movement, historian William Sturkey writes that white claims to commitment based on their visible participation outlived their actual, ongoing commitments; then as now, public opinion changed, but "everyone claimed to have been a civil rights activist."[67] There have always been committed white anti-racists—well-known and lesser known—whose solidarity, support, and accountability to people of color movements organizations can serve as inspiration.[68] History shows us, however, that broad-based white support for racial justice tends to be fleeting.

This suggests the need for a more sustained, more serious consideration of what community accountability means—not just for those who cause harm in criminalized and racialized communities, not just in cases of police violence—but for everyday white people. The need was evidenced before the decline of white support for Black Lives Matter: What was the role of all those white people in meetings about community alternatives to policing in Black neighborhoods? White people can and do play a role in holding the police accountable, organizing around city police budgets, watching and documenting police activity, creating civilian review boards, doing legislative work to ban violent practices, and supporting neighbors. These are all commitments that could be construed as part of a white accountability process. Beyond signaling that one is "on the right side of history," transformative whiteness puts white people collectively in the role of having caused harm, and collectively in the position of seeking healing, repair, redress, and transformation for that harm and the conditions that gave rise to it. While there may certainly be feelings involved in such work, "be warned" Kaba writes, "that there will be no magical day of liberation that *we* do not make."[69] Transforming the conditions in which we "live, work, and play such that prolonged racial harm doesn't occur" is our work to do, and if we are white, that work is both necessary and highly contradictory.

As we have seen, guilt, shame, and blame are maladaptive responses that tend to reproduce the denials and deflections of white ignorance. As Aurora Levins Morales writes, feeling helpless in the face of widespread harm or abuse—like the harms of racism, capitalism, and other kinds of exploitation—can lead to "militarization, to extreme nationalism, to the kind of opportunism that's willing to win some kind of sovereignty or security for our own group at the expense of others—which of course only continues the cycle, creates new groups of desperate people."[70] Levins Morales is describing the seeming inevitability of the punishment paradigm, the helplessness and paralysis we saw described by psychologists in chapter 3, the aggrievement and defensiveness that is the hegemonic expression of whiteness.

But white people are in no way helpless when it comes to participating in racial harm. White people can certainly challenge white supremacy, colonialism, and imperialism. They can, and do, in classrooms, workplaces, families, neighborhoods, relationships, political organizations, and within themselves. Transformative whiteness suggests an open political process beyond "anti-bias training" that, as the principles of transformative justice hold, addresses the conditions of harm, thereby transforming it. Rather than simply "unlearning anti-Indigenous bias," for example, transformative whiteness would address the land dispossession and lack of regard for treaty rights and self-determination, following the lead of Indigenous organizers. As George Manuel has written, anti-Indigenous racism will only come to an end when that land is given back, and reparations are paid.[71] Education and the development of political consciousness are essential for white people to awaken to their role as colonizers, but it is not the end goal, as the contemporary #LandBack movement also demonstrates.[72] The goal is to actively make way for a process of non-white self-determination that will transform the conditions of colonial racial-capitalism into something new.

NOTES

1. Kenneth Jones and Tema Okun, *Dismantling Racism: A Workbook for Social Change Groups* (Changework, 2001), https://resourcegeneration.org/wp-content/uploads/2018/01/2016-dRworks-workbook.pdf.
2. Mark B. Brown, "James Baldwin and the Politics of White Identity," *Contemporary Political Theory*, May 4, 2020, https://doi.org/10.1057/s41296-020-00401-9.
3. Courtenay W. Daum, "White Complicity," *New Political Science* 42, no. 3 (July 2, 2020): 443–49, https://doi.org/10.1080/07393148.2020.1817673.
4. Ibid.
5. Ibid.
6. Timothy Wyman McCarty, "Insisting on Complicity," *Contemporary Political Theory* 18, no. 1 (March 1, 2019): 1–21, 3.
7. Ibid.
8. Ibid.
9. Christopher Kutz, *Complicity: Ethics and Law for a Collective Age* (Cambridge: Cambridge University Press, 2007).
10. Barbara Applebaum, *Being White, Being Good: White Complicity, White Moral Responsibility, and Social Justice Pedagogy* (Lexington Books, 2010), 125.
11. Applebaum, 129.
12. Ibid.
13. Kutz, *Complicity*.
14. Ibid., 113.
15. Kutz, *Complicity*.
16. Ibid., 258.
17. Chiara Lepora and Robert E. Goodin, *On Complicity and Compromise* (OUP Oxford, 2013).

18. Ibid., 96.

19. Larry May, *Sharing Responsibility* (University of Chicago Press, 1996).

20. Alison Bailey, "Taking Responsibility for Community Violence," in *Feminists Doing Ethics*, 2001, https://papers.ssrn.com/abstract=1394418.

21. Bailey.

22. Applebaum, *Being White, Being Good.*

23. Some philosophers like Gregory Mellema have distinguished between "moral taint" and complicity. For Mellema, complicity necessarily involves an active contribution, whereas moral taint can arise from non-causal associations with moral wrong. See

24. Kutz's account also stresses relationality and positionality, and among recent research on complicity, is the most promising. Kutz rejects "retributive" models as solipsistic and neglecting the collective and relational context for human action. For Kutz, agency is necessarily participatory (Kutz 2000, 11).

25. Applebaum, *Being White, Being Good,* 3.

26. Ibid.

27. Ibid.

28. Ibid., 15.

29. Barbara Applebaum, "In the Name of Morality: Moral Responsibility, Whiteness and Social Justice Education," *Journal of Moral Education* 34, no. 3 (September 1, 2005): 277–90, https://doi.org/10.1080/03057240500206089.

30. Applebaum, *Being White, Being Good,* 14.

31. Also taken up by Applebaum, who sees it as consistent with white complicity pedagogy.

32. Arendt differentiated between liability and blame, claiming that while not all those who participated in German society were to blame, they could nonetheless be considered liable. Young merges these into the liability model, and I have followed that move in this chapter.

33. Hannah Arendt, "Collective Responsibility," in *Amor Mundi: Explorations in the Faith and Thought of Hannah Arendt*, ed. S. J. James W. Bernauer, Boston College Studies in Philosophy (Dordrecht: Springer Netherlands, 1987), 43–50, 47.

34. There is much to be said about the use of the analogy between the Holocaust and anti-Black racism in the US. While some Jewish activists have used the slogan "Never Again is Now" during the Trump administration, and have participated in the most recent racial justice uprisings under the name Never Again Action, scholar Ben Ratskoff writes that this "victim bonding" can obscure the complicity of white Jews in white supremacy. (See https://jewishcurrents.org/against-analogy/) Of course, this is meant to trace the limits of the analogy, not to deny the reality and particular structural role played by anti-Semitism in our contemporary context, or to deny the reality of Black Jews, non-white Jews, Sephardi and Misrahi Jews, and Jews of Color, who do not benefit from white supremacy in the way that white Ashkenazi Jews do.

35. Iris Marion Young, *Responsibility for Justice* (Oxford University Press, 2010).

36. Young.

37. Iris Marion Young, "Responsibility and Global Justice: A Social Connection Model ," *Social Philosophy and Policy* 23, no. 1 (January 2006): 102–30, 102–3.

38. "Contributing by their actions" is broad enough to include those whose actions may not make a "difference to the difference," and whose actions may not have been intentional. In this sense, the SCM is different from the accounts of complicity critiqued above.

39. Young, "RESPONSIBILITY AND GLOBAL JUSTICE," 114.

40. Young's SCM has been critiqued by some who take complicity to inhibit the acknowledgement of social connection and our embeddedness in social and political relations. Jacob Schiff takes the acknowledgement of "the normal as problematic" and the acknowledgement of the fact of social connection to be limitations of Young's account. It is true that Young did not have the opportunity to fully expand the SCM to account for these epistemic and motivational dimensions. But her finding normativity beyond character, causality, affect, and intention has obvious merits for addressing white ignorance. See Jacob Schiff, "Confronting Political Responsibility: The Problem of Acknowledgment," *Hypatia* 23, no. 3 (2008): 99–117.

41. Which of course is not the same as the kind of "political eliminativism" that aims to *eventually*, *collectively* end whiteness and white supremacy—a goal that is remote, if compelling.

42. Sharon D. Welch, *A Feminist Ethic of Risk* (Fortress Press, 1990), 73.

43. Boaventura de Sousa Santos, *Epistemologies of the South: Justice Against Epistemicide* (Routledge, 2015).

44. Mariame Kaba and Shira Hassan, *Fumbling Towards Repair: A Workbook for Community Accountability Facilitators* (PROJECT NIA, 2019).

45. Shannon Perez-Darby, "The Secret Joys of Accountability," in Ching-In Chen, Jai Dulani, and Leah Lakshmi Piepzna-Samarasinha, eds., *The Revolution Starts at Home: Confronting Intimate Violence Within Activist Communities*, 2016.

46. Ibid., 107.

47. Young, "RESPONSIBILITY AND GLOBAL JUSTICE," 112.

48. Intimate violence, in the case of Perez-Darby's work.

49. Perez-Darby, in Chen, Dulani, and Piepzna-Samarasinha, *The Revolution Starts at Home,* 110.

50. Justice work should have liberation as its goal. But this characterization of Young's is particularly apt for avoiding white vanguardism that might set goals without taking relational or racial position into account.

51. José Medina, *The Epistemology of Resistance: Gender and Racial Oppression, Epistemic Injustice, and Resistant Imaginations* (Oxford: Oxford University Press, 2012); Sara Ahmed, *On Being Included: Racism and Diversity in Institutional Life* (Duke University Press, 2012).

52. Medina, *The Epistemology of Resistance*; Santos, *Epistemologies of the South.*

53. Welch, *A Feminist Ethic of Risk,* 73.

54. Ernesto Javier Martínez, *On Making Sense: Queer Race Narratives of Intelligibility* (Stanford University Press, 2012), 51.

55. Mariana Ortega, *In-Between: Latina Feminist Phenomenology, Multiplicity, and the Self,* reprint edition (Albany: State University of New York Press, 2016).

56. Recently, some right wing groups like Hobby Lobby have sought to prove their complicity with "sin" in order to opt out of laws requiring companies to provide

health benefits that could allow employees to get an abortion. Hobby Lobby's goal in pursuing complicity in the courts was to receive an accommodation to opt out of the laws alleged to be making them "sinfully complicit" (McCarty 2019). Where this case of "political complicity aims to disengage and disavow, complicity responsibility aims, when possible, to maintain complicit relations and associations in order to engage in transformative, non-punitive, anti-racist work.

57. Larry May and Cassie Striblen have both argued that vocal disapproval can counteract one's complicity and restore one's moral standing. Howard McGary has written that complicity can be resolved through the "dissociation condition" when one removes oneself from the conditions of harm. May, *Sharing Responsibility*; Cassie Striblen, "Guilt, Shame, and Shared Responsibility," *Journal of Social Philosophy* 38 (August 7, 2007): 469–85; Howard McGary, "Morality and Collective Liability," *The Journal of Value Inquiry* 20, no. 2 (June 1, 1986): 157–65.

58. For McGary, dissent or disavowal of normalized racism remove one's complicity.

59. Michele Anderson, "Opinion | Go Home to Your 'Dying' Hometown," *The New York Times*, March 8, 2019, sec. Opinion, https://www.nytimes.com/2019/03/08/opinion/sunday/urban-rural-america.html.

60. Shira Hassan and Mimi Kim, "Modern Roots of Transformative Justice," Barnard Center for Research on Women, October 13, 2020, https://bcrw.barnard.edu/videos/modern-roots-of-transformative-justice/.

61. Charles V. Hamilton and Kwame Ture, *Black Power: Politics of Liberation in America* (Knopf Doubleday Publishing Group, 2011), 82.

62. Ibid.

63. Ibid.

64. Mia Mingus, "Transformative Justice: A Brief Description," *Transform Harm* (blog), January 11, 2019, https://transformharm.org/transformative-justice-a-brief-description/.

65. Chen, Dulani, and Piepzna-Samarasinha, *The Revolution Starts at Home*.

66. Erin Logan, "White People Have Gentrified Black Lives Matter. It's a Problem," *Los Angeles Times*, September 4, 2020, sec. Opinion, https://www.latimes.com/opinion/story/2020-09-04/black-lives-matter-white-people-portland-protests-nfl.

67. Ibid.

68. See, among many others: Marilyn Buck, *Inside/Out: Selected Poems* (City Lights Publishers, 2012); David Gilbert and Boots Riley, *Love and Struggle: My Life in SDS, the Weather Underground, and Beyond*, 2011; Mab Segrest, *Memoir of a Race Traitor: Fighting Racism in the American South*, 2019; Chris Crass, Chris Dixon, and Roxanne Dunbar-Ortiz, *Towards Collective Liberation: Anti-Racist Organizing, Feminist Praxis, and Movement Building Strategy*, 2013.

69. Mariame Kaba, *We Do This 'Til We Free Us: Abolitionist Organizing and Transforming Justice* (Haymarket Books, 2021), 138.

70. Kaba and Hassan, *Fumbling Towards Repair*, 8.

71. George Manuel and Michael Posluns, *The Fourth World: An Indian Reality* (University of Minnesota Press, 2019), 221–222.

72. "LANDBACK," LANDBACK, accessed July 15, 2021, https://landback.org/.

Conclusion

Against White Success

This is a book about how we respond to harm. By linking the construction of whiteness to the politics and morality of punishment and absolution, it raised the problem of white responsibility for racial harm that so frequently reproduces that harm in its very attempts to account for it. It established the collective nature of white racial harm and its benefits for white people as a problem for mainstream moral frameworks, since these approaches tend to focus on individuals' causal contributions, intentions, and knowledge of the facts in order to determine accountability. In the case of white supremacy and white dominance, however, harm is perpetuated through cumulative, aggregate actions that may or may not be caused, intended, or cognized by individuals. This is true even as white people engage in the active reproduction of whiteness through their habits and behaviors, and derive enormous material, moral, emotional, and political benefit from that reproduction at the expense of non-white and colonized people. Moral frameworks that frame harm as the result of causal contributions, bad intentions, correct affect, or self-awareness tend to understand accountability as the attribution of blame or absolution: one is innocent or guilty, good or bad.

The dilemma is that these binary, punitive, individualizing moralities are bound up with processes of racialization, and thus have difficulty capturing responsibility for collective harms like white ignorance. Not only do they have trouble justifying them, they reproduce that harm by encouraging white people to seek moral absolution, innocence, and the purification of moral taint instead of addressing the material conditions of harm: namely, land dispossession, colonization, imperialism, the ongoing extractivism and exploitation of racial capitalism. By landing on the notions of complicit responsibility and transformative whiteness, this book aimed to circumvent the binary, purity-seeking, punitive responses to harm that reproduce white ignorance.

This book claimed the space of complicity as a place of anti-racist possibility, aiming to get around the fatalistic notion that white anti-racism is impossible—the faulty notion that because either "all are guilty" or none are, there can be no white responsibility for racial harm. I rejected that fatalism on the grounds that collective responsibility for racial harm is not synonymous with either guilt or innocence, but a complicit, non-transcendent process of mitigating and resisting white supremacy based on the social and political roles that position us to work in and across our communities. Rather than fixating on individuals' moral status as guilty, innocent, blame or praise-worthy while abstracting away from the material conditions of racial harm, I advocated for an other-regarding, future-oriented approach that takes white racial complicity as a given as long as racial capitalism exists. Instead of understanding responsibility as the cleansing of moral taint, I made the case for a different way of responding to harm as necessary for dismantling the moral, racial, political, and affective constructs that keep racial capitalism in place.

The book began by showing in chapter 1 that white ignorance is a special kind of denial, a "need not to know" that aggressively resists acknowledging the role of race and racism. That denial is hegemonic: it dominates our political landscape, warps our moral frameworks (chapter 2) and our affective responses (chapter 3), intervenes in our self-conceptions, and organizes our identities. In this sense, white ignorance is a structuring form that generates responses to harm that reproduce that harm. This is because the deflection undertaken by white ignorance serves the preservation of white moral capital and moral standing; white ignorance is the means to both white innocence and white material and political appropriation and dominance. This keeps racializing structures and institutions in place through an epistemology of aggrieved denial that refuses to acknowledge the racist *raison d'être* of those institutions, while protecting white people from that "troubling recognition."[1] It is in that sense that white ignorance is the epistemological dimension of white supremacy; it is a "twilight state" of simultaneous knowing and not knowing that protects white people and white institutions from the knowledge that would expose the violence of its dominance and the racial harm of normalized white benefit.

The implication of this is that in order to shift the persistent white tendency to "see the world wrongly" in the face of the blatant facts of racial harm, we will have to address the conditions the produce it. This is to say that a transformed whiteness depends not only on attitudinal changes and the promotion of "facts" about racism, but on literal, non-metaphorical transformative *justice*. If white settler moralities are punitive, as chapters 2 and 3 showed, then our moral responses are bound up with power, belonging, and racial politics. Given the entanglement of our moral and racial concepts with the differential allocation of life chances and access to material resources, we cannot have transformative whiteness without broad transformative responses to harm—without transformative justice.

The idea of transformative whiteness can help us get around the false dilemma of racial essentialism that sees eliminativism—the abolition or wholesale repudiation of whiteness—as the only solution to the problem of white dominance. Because whiteness is not an incontrovertible racial essence, but is constructed by the political and economic relations, norms, and institutions described in the chapters of this book, the problems of whiteness and white supremacy can only be addressed by remaking those relations and dismantling those institutions.

This means ending the prison industrial complex that criminalizes race while defending white civic innocence; ending a punitive, white supremacist education system that inculcates students with the capitalist values of race and class exploitation and obedient work at all costs; ending the dominance of the insurance industry and finance capital over our care, health, shelter, and safety and its parasitism on poor and racialized people; abolishing the police and policing as manifestations of white violence, aggrievement, and racist control; ending the repression of colonized people around the world, returning land, and respecting self-determination; and destabilizing ideologies of salvation and purity that reproduce white notions of mastery. Insofar as each of these forms of harm is a deflection, reversal, or obfuscation of racialized exploitation and dispossession, each is an example of white ignorance, and each merits a complicit, transformative response. Each is an expression of white supremacy, normalized by white ignorance, which is sustained by them in turn. If white ignorance is the epistemic dimension of white supremacy, then responsibility for it requires far more than knowledge acquisition or a shift in attitude. The condition for cognitive, epistemic change is the active, imaginative construction of new institutions and new ways of being that will transform the conditions of racial harm.

I am writing this conclusion during a moment of real imagination and possibility regarding how we respond to harm. Since the 2020 uprisings, "abolition" and "transformative justice" have become household terms, and the idea of eliminating prisons and policing is no longer considered a fantasy of the ultra-left fringe, but discussed in the mainstream media. On the left and in movement spaces, complex, creative conversations are taking place that aim to address the reproduction of racism, sexism and ableism without relying on punishment or state institutions, and without making anyone disposable. For those of us interested in forms of accountability that break cycles of violence, this is an exciting time. Strong voices in the movement are agitating against binary moralities that assume the impossibility of change for individuals, groups, ecosystems, and establishing transformation as a new paradigm. We are in a moment of courageous reckoning, not just about race and racism, but about what responsibility and accountability mean in theory and practice, about the limits of punishment and retribution, and the value of recognizing vulnerability, difference, and the capacity to make mistakes. Malkia Devich Cyril observes that our movements can model a new kind of accountability. As they write,

> it requires great honesty to admit that innocence is an imagined narrative created to deny everyone agency, and to set up those who cross lines and cause harm as deviant outliers, exceptions to humanity's rule. Especially when even a modest look inside one's own history reveals that every hand has dirt on it. . . . While all harms are not equal, even the most heinous require a way home.[2]

Devich Cyril is not rejecting "call outs"—the use of our voices to denounce violence or the reproduction of harm. But they are agitating for complexity and humanity in the ways that we address the forms of oppression that structure our world and inhabit our relationships and organizing spaces. To recognize that all human beings have the capacity to harm, and the capacity to change themselves and their world, is the epistemic commitment of transformative whiteness.

Transformative whiteness is meant both to describe the flexibility of whiteness as a category, and the possibilities of inhabiting of the paradoxical space of white accountability. It is not meant to be a rubric, checklist, or theory of change, but one tool among many for circumventing the punishment paradigm's reproduction of harm by acknowledging and accepting complicity. It is a guiding idea, a wish, an experimental proposal, and an adaptation of important work done in other contexts. But it does not promise to be an easy experiment. If white ignorance collectively puts white people in a position of complicity where they "see the world wrongly," then they will be compromised in their ability to determine the shape racial justice should take. That position of compromise, friction, and complicity is where transformative whiteness can begin. In order to transform our institutions, our relationships, and ourselves, whiteness needs to be detached from its entitlement to the relief of absolution and innocence, from its essentialization as pure and good—and, conversely, its paralyzing essentialization as bad. Models of responsibility for racism that fixate on guilt and innocence are not just a category mistake, mistaking a collective problem for an individual one; they are also *anti*-accountable in motivating the preservation of good, innocent whiteness, that operates with the "correct" sensibility and affect, and re-centers white people as paradigm moral actors in the face of wrong, while paralyzing them when it comes to the work of making change in the world.

For these reasons, we need alternative frameworks for responsibility for racism and white ignorance that don't aim for moral purity or white success, but take white failure and complicity as a natural and inevitable part of a long term process of transformation. This kind of approach puts aside the desire to transcend or escape the harm we participate in, and should closely examine white narratives of beleaguerment and victimhood as places for transformative political education. The transformative justice approach has resources for us to make this shift away from anti-accountable, punitive whiteness that maintains that responding to harm is a matter of restoring individual moral worth. Transformative justice, for example, while it does identify harm caused, rejects the idea of pure victims and perpetrators, where the goal of the process is to determine what kind of punishment or suffering is in order for the perpetrator of harm. Rather, transformative justice recognizes the impact of the harm on all parties involved, asking, "Are we figuring out what both the person who has harmed and the person who has caused harm need in order to heal? Or are we trying to replicate the same pain and humiliation that happened when the initial harm took place?"[3]

Developing a new paradigm for responding to white collective harm thus requires abandoning the notion of white success. Committing to transformative justice is committing to a process, not a verdict on guilt or innocence. From this point of view, white "rightness" and success are natural to want, but are not an appropriate focus for addressing white ignorance. As transformative justice practitioners Jenna Peters-Golden and Bench Ansfield write, "success is conventionally understood as signifying completion and resolution, as opposed to reflecting the jumble of small victories, uncertainties, and defeats that typify organizing work."[4] While feelings of guilt may motivate us to seek resolution for structural racism, white people are setting themselves up for frustration, resentment, and disappointment—negative affects in response to issues of race that can manifest as racism—when this resolution doesn't materialize (and it likely will not in our lifetimes). Transformative justice models of accountability can help us with the seeming trap of white responsibility for racism by holding that "there is no such thing as a 'successful' accountability process."[5] Rather, the goal and hope of an accountability process is "to mitigate the impact of the harm that has occurred, and prevent it from happening again."[6] Success presumes that "there is a way to undo the harm that has occurred." But the harms of structural racism cannot be undone, and healing will have to accept the ongoing reality and consequences of that harm.

A framework of responsibility that isn't focused on white success can be more focused on transformation through accountability. This means circumventing the question of blame for structural harm in favor of frameworks that motivate white people to change their behaviors, relationships, and institutions. Punishment—which we have seen is tied to whiteness—deems someone worthy of retribution, revenge, or suffering. Punishment is received passively, and in that sense, is unaccountable.[7] Accountability, by contrast, is an active willingness to accept the consequences of one's actions and involvements. If we are going to take collective responsibility for structural racism, white people should develop models of accountability that are active engagements with the ongoing harm in which they participate, rather than models that punish whiteness as an unchangeable fact.[8] That white passivity only allows for the reproduction of racism—even if active uptake also necessarily runs that risk. The racialization of punishment demands that we develop frameworks of responsibility that decenter white innocence, even in that active uptake. These alternative models would do well to inhabit the contradiction of white anti-racist agency by centering those most directly impacted by racism. Cultivating that agency is an active process—not passive waiting—that deliberately shifts the self-centering habits of whiteness. As Kazu Haga writes, "without creating intentional and alternative structures that allow us to practice operating differently, we inevitably revert back to the same ways of relating to each other that got us into this mess."[9] White people owe themselves and others the respect and humanity to do and be otherwise.

NOTES

1. Stanley Cohen, *States of Denial: Knowing about Atrocities and Suffering* (John Wiley &and Sons, 2013); Christopher Bollas, *Being a Character: Psychoanalysis and Self Experience* (Psychology Press, 1993).

2. adrienne maree brown, *We Will Not Cancel Us: And Other Dreams of Transformative Justice* (AK Press, 2020), 85.

3. Mariame Kaba and Shira Hassan, *Fumbling Towards Repair: A Workbook for Community Accountability Facilitators* (PROJECT NIA, 2019).

4. Bench Ansfield and Jenna Peters-Golden, "How We Learned Not to Succeed in Transformative Justice," *Make/Shift Magazine: Feminisms in Motion* 12 (March 2012).

5. Ibid.

6. Ibid.

7. Kaba and Hassan, *Fumbling Towards Repair*.

8. This would also require white people to actively distinguish between punishment and consequences. As Robin DiAngelo has shown, there is a white tendency to respond to consequences as if they were punishments. Robin DiAngelo and Michael Eric Dyson, *White Fragility: Why It's So Hard for White People to Talk About Racism*, Reprint edition (Boston: Beacon Press, 2018).

9. Kazu Haga, *Healing Resistance: A Radically Different Response to Harm* (Parallax Press, 2020).

Bibliography

Accapadi, Mamta Motwani. "When White Women Cry: How White Women's Tears Oppress Women of Color." *College Student Affairs Journal* 26, no. 2 (2007): 208–15.

Ahmed, Sara. "Declarations of Whiteness: The Non-Performativity of Anti-Racism." *Borderlands* 3, no. 2 (2004). http://www.borderlands.net.au/vol3no2_2004/ahmed_declarations.htm.

———. *On Being Included: Racism and Diversity in Institutional Life*. Duke University Press, 2012.

Alcoff, Linda. "How Critical Race Theory Became the New Conservative Bogeyman." *The Indypendent*, May 25, 2021. https://indypendent.org/2021/05/how-critical-race-theory-became-the-new-conservative-bogeyman/.

Alcoff, Linda Martín. "Epistemologies of Ignorance: Three Types." In *Race and Epistemologies of Ignorance*, edited by Nancy Tuana and Shannon Sullivan, 39–57. Albany: SUNY Press, 2012.

———. *The Future of Whiteness*. John Wiley & Sons, 2015.

Alexander, M. Jacqui. *Pedagogies of Crossing: Meditations on Feminism, Sexual Politics, Memory, and the Sacred.* Duke University Press, 2006.

Amodio, David M., Patricia G. Devine, and Eddie Harmon-Jones. "A Dynamic Model of Guilt: Implications for Motivation and Self-Regulation in the Context of Prejudice." *Psychological Science* 18, no. 6 (June 2007): 524–30. https://doi.org/10.1111/j.1467-9280.2007.01933.x.

Anderson, Michele. "Opinion | Go Home to Your 'Dying' Hometown." *The New York Times*, March 8, 2019, sec. Opinion. https://www.nytimes.com/2019/03/08/opinion/sunday/urban-rural-america.html.

Ansfield, Bench, and Jenna Peters-Golden. "How We Learned Not to Succeed in Transformative Justice." *Make/Shift Magazine: Feminisms in Motion* 12 (March 2012).

Aouragh, Miriyam. "'White Privilege' and Shortcuts to Anti-Racism." *Race & Class* 61, no. 2 (October 1, 2019): 3–26. https://doi.org/10.1177/0306396819874629.

Applebaum, Barbara. *Being White, Being Good: White Complicity, White Moral Responsibility, and Social Justice Pedagogy*. Lexington Books, 2010.

———. "In the Name of Morality: Moral Responsibility, Whiteness and Social Justice Education." *Journal of Moral Education* 34, no. 3 (September 1, 2005): 277–90. https://doi.org/10.1080/03057240500206089.

Arendt, Hannah. "Collective Responsibility." In *Amor Mundi: Explorations in the Faith and Thought of Hannah Arendt*, edited by S. J. James W. Bernauer, 43–50. Boston College Studies in Philosophy. Dordrecht: Springer Netherlands, 1987. https://doi.org/10.1007/978-94-009-3565-5_3.

Aronson, Brittany A. "The White Savior Industrial Complex: A Cultural Studies Analysis of a Teacher Educator, Savior Film, and Future Teachers." *Journal of Critical Thought and Praxis* 6, no. 3 (2017): 9270485. https://doi.org/10.31274/jctp-180810-83.

Bailey, Alison. "'Strategic Ignorance.'" In *Race and Epistemologies of Ignorance*, edited by Nancy Tuana and Shannon Sullivan, 77–95. Albany: SUNY Press, 2012.

———. "'White Talk' as a Barrier to Understanding Whiteness." In *White Self-Criticality Beyond Anti-Racism: How Does It Feel to Be a White Problem?*, edited by George Yancy, 37–57. Lexington Books, 2014.

Baldwin, James. "A Letter to My Nephew." *Progressive.Org*, December 1, 1962. https://progressive.org/%3Fq%3Dnews/2014/12/5047/letter-my-nephew/.

———. "On Being 'White'. . . And Other Lies." In *Black On White: Black Writers on What It Means to Be White*. New York: Schocken Books, 1998.

———. *The Price of the Ticket: Collected Nonfiction, 1948–1985*. Macmillan, 1985.

Baldwin, James, and Edward P. Jones. *Notes of a Native Son*. 1st edition. Boston: Beacon Press, 2012.

Bartky, Sandra Lee. *Sympathy and Solidarity: And Other Essays*. Rowman & Littlefield, 2002.

Bell, Derrick. *Faces At The Bottom Of The Well: The Permanence Of Racism*. Basic Books, 1992.

Berenstain, Nora. "Epistemic Exploitation." *Ergo, an Open Access Journal of Philosophy* 3 (2016). https://doi.org/10.3998/ergo.12405314.0003.022.

Berg, Philip L. "Racism and the Puritan Mind." *Phylon (1960–)* 36, no. 1 (1975): 1–7.

Berger, Dan. *The Struggle Within: Prisons, Political Prisoners, and Mass Movements in the United States*. PM Press, 2014.

Berila, Beth. "White Urgency to End Racism: Why Now?" *OpenDemocracy*. Accessed July 6, 2021. https://www.opendemocracy.net/en/transformation/white-urgency-end-racism-why-now/.

Berlet, Chip. *Eyes Right!: Challenging the Right Wing Backlash*. South End Press, 1995.

Bobo, Lawrence, Camille Charles, Maria Krysan, and Alicia Simmons. "The Real Record on Racial Attitudes." In *Social Trends in American Life: Findings from the General Social Survey since 1972*, edited by Peter V. Marsden. Princeton, NJ: Princeton University Press, 2012.

Bollas, Christopher. *Being a Character: Psychoanalysis and Self Experience*. Psychology Press, 1993.

Bonilla-Silva, Eduardo. *Racism without Racists: Color-Blind Racism and the Persistence of Racial Inequality in the United States*. Rowman & Littlefield Publishers, 2006.

Boyd, Dwight R. *Becoming of Two Minds about Liberalism: A Chronicle of Philosophical and Moral Development*. Springer, 2015.

Brodkin, Karen. *How Jews Became White Folks and What That Says about Race in America*. Rutgers University Press, 1998.

brown, adrienne maree. *We Will Not Cancel Us: And Other Dreams of Transformative Justice*. AK Press, 2020.

Brown, Jericho. *The Tradition*. Copper Canyon Press, 2019.

Buck, Marilyn. *Inside/Out: Selected Poems*. City Lights Publishers, 2012.

Camp, Jordan T. *Incarcerating the Crisis: Freedom Struggles and the Rise of the Neoliberal State*. University of California Press, 2016.

Césaire, Aimé. *Discourse on Colonialism*. NYU Press, 2001.

Chen, Ching-In, Jai Dulani, and Leah Lakshmi Piepzna-Samarasinha, eds. *The Revolution Starts at Home: Confronting Intimate Violence Within Activist Communities*, 2016.

Coates, Ta-Nehisi. *Between the World and Me*. Spiegel & Grau, 2015.

Cohen, Stanley. *States of Denial: Knowing about Atrocities and Suffering*. John Wiley & Sons, 2013.

Cole, Teju. "The White-Savior Industrial Complex—The Atlantic." Accessed May 26, 2021. https://www.theatlantic.com/international/archive/2012/03/the-white-savior-industrial-complex/254843/.

Coulthard, Glen Sean. *Red Skin, White Masks: Rejecting the Colonial Politics of Recognition*. University of Minnesota Press, 2014.

Craig, Maureen A., and Jennifer A. Richeson. "On the Precipice of a 'Majority-Minority' America: Perceived Status Threat From the Racial Demographic Shift Affects White Americans' Political Ideology." *Psychological Science* 25, no. 6 (June 1, 2014): 1189–97. https://doi.org/10.1177/0956797614527113.

Crass, Chris, Chris Dixon, and Roxanne Dunbar-Ortiz. *Towards Collective Liberation: Anti-Racist Organizing, Feminist Praxis, and Movement Building Strategy*, 2013.

Crenshaw, Kimberle. "Mapping the Margins: Intersectionality, Identity Politics, and Violence against Women of Color." *Stanford Law Review* 43, no. 6 (1991): 1241–99. https://doi.org/10.2307/1229039.

The Chronicle of Higher Education. "Race, Ethnicity, and Gender of Full-Time Faculty Members at More Than 3,400 Institutions.," May 21, 2021. https://www.chronicle.com/article/race-ethnicity-and-gender-of-full-time-faculty-at-more-than-3-700-institutions/.

Daum, Courtenay W. "White Complicity." *New Political Science* 42, no. 3 (July 2, 2020): 443–49. https://doi.org/10.1080/07393148.2020.1817673.

Delgado, Richard, Jean Stefancic, and Foreword Angela Harris. "From Critical Race Theory: An Introduction." In *NYU Press*, 6, 2006.

DiAngelo, Robin, and Michael Eric Dyson. *White Fragility: Why It's So Hard for White People to Talk About Racism*. Reprint edition. Boston: Beacon Press, 2018.

Dilts, Andrew. *Punishment and Inclusion: Race, Membership, and the Limits of American Liberalism*. Fordham University Press, 2014.

Du Bois, W. E. B. *Black Reconstruction in America: Toward a History of the Part Which Black Folk Played in the Attempt to Reconstruct Democracy in America, 1860-1880*. Transaction Publishers, 2013.

———. "The African Roots of War." *Monthly Review* 24, no. 11 (April 3, 1973): 28. https://doi.org/10.14452/MR-024-11-1973-04_3.

Du Bois, W. E. B. "Marxism and the Negro Problem:: W E B Du Bois. Org." *The Crisis*, 1933.

Farid, Mujahid, and Laura Whitehorn. "Release Aging People in Prison (RAPP): Challenging the Punishment Paradigm." *Socialism and Democracy* 28, no. 3 (September 2, 2014): 199–202. https://doi.org/10.1080/08854300.2014.957590.

Feagin, Joe R., Hernán Vera Lamperein, Hernan Vera, and Pinar Batur. *White Racism: The Basics*. Psychology Press, 2001.

Fensterwald, John. "A Final Vote, after Many Rewrites, for California's Controversial Ethnic Studies Curriculum." *EdSource*, March 17, 2021. https://edsource.org/2021/a-final-vote-after-many-rewrites-for-californias-controversial-ethnic-studies-curriculum/651338.

Frankenberg, Ruth. *White Women, Race Matters: The Social Construction of Whiteness*. Minneapolis: University of Minnesota Press, 1993.

Fricker, Miranda. *Epistemic Injustice: Power and the Ethics of Knowing*. Clarendon Press, 2007.

Galgay, Corinne E. "Affective Costs of Whiteness: Examining the Role of White Guilt and White Shame." Columbia University, 2018. file:///C:/Users/boodman/Downloads/Galgay_columbia_0054D_14884.pdf.

Gerbner, Katharine. *Christian Slavery: Conversion and Race in the Protestant Atlantic World*. University of Pennsylvania Press, 2018.

Ghandnoosh, Nazgol. "Race and Punishment: Racial Perceptions of Crime and Support for Punitive Policies." Sentencing Project, September 3, 2014. https://www.sentencingproject.org/publications/race-and-punishment-racial-perceptions-of-crime-and-support-for-punitive-policies/.

Gilbert, David, and Boots Riley. *Love and Struggle: My Life in SDS, the Weather Underground, and Beyond*, 2011.

Gilmore, Ruth Wilson. *Golden Gulag: Prisons, Surplus, Crisis, and Opposition in Globalizing California*. University of California Press, 2007.

Giridharadas, Anand. "The January 6 Insurrection Was a Last Gasp for White Supremacy." Accessed May 11, 2021. https://www.msnbc.com/the-last-word/watch/the-january-6-insurrection-was-a-last-gasp-for-white-supremacy-99557445706.

Gray, Matt. "Cop Who Shot and Killed Black N.J. Teen in 1994 Should Be Fired from University Post, Family Says." NJ.com, June 8, 2020, sec. Gloucester County. https://www.nj.com/gloucester-county/2020/06/cop-who-shot-and-killed-black-nj-teen-in-1994-should-be-fired-from-university-post-family-says.html.

Haga, Kazu. *Healing Resistance: A Radically Different Response to Harm*. Parallax Press, 2020.

Hamilton, Charles V., and Kwame Ture. *Black Power: Politics of Liberation in America*. Knopf Doubleday Publishing Group, 2011.

Harris, Cheryl I. "Whiteness as Property." *Harvard Law Review* 106, no. 8 (1993): 1707–91. https://doi.org/10.2307/1341787.

Hassan, Shira, and Mimi Kim. "Modern Roots of Transformative Justice." Barnard Center for Research on Women, October 13, 2020. https://bcrw.barnard.edu/videos/modern-roots-of-transformative-justice/.

Hochschild, Arlie Russell. *Strangers in Their Own Land: Anger and Mourning on the American Right*. The New Press, 2016.

Horne, Gerald. *The Dawning of the Apocalypse: The Roots of Slavery, White Supremacy, Settler Colonialism, and Capitalism in the Long Sixteenth Century*. NYU Press, 2020.

Hughey, Matthew. "The (Dis)Similarities of White Racial Identities: The Conceptual Framework of 'Hegemonic Whiteness'"; *Ethnic and Racial Studies* 33, no. 8 (n.d.): 1289–1309.

———. *White Bound: Nationalists, Antiracists, and the Shared Meanings of Race*. Stanford University Press, 2012.

Hutchins-Newman, Ariane. "White Faculty Perceptions of Diversity and Diversity Work." Rowan University, 2019.

Ignatiev, Noel. *How the Irish Became White*. Routledge, 2012.

INCITE!, INCITE! Women of Color Against Violence. *The Revolution Will Not Be Funded: Beyond the Non-Profit Industrial Complex*. Duke University Press, 2017.

Indigenous Action Media. "Accomplices Not Allies: Abolishing the Ally Industrial Complex." *Indigenous Action Media* (blog), May 4, 2014. https://www.indigenousaction.org/accomplices-not-allies-abolishing-the-ally-industrial-complex/.

Ioanide, Paula. "Defensive Appropriations." In *Antiracism Inc.: Why the Way We Talk about Racial Justice Matters*, edited by Felice Blake, Alison Reed, and Paula Ioanide, 83–107. Brooklyn, NY: punctum books, 2019.

———. *The Emotional Politics of Racism: How Feelings Trump Facts in an Era of Colorblindness*. Stanford University Press, 2015.

James, Joy. *The New Abolitionists: (Neo)Slave Narratives and Contemporary Prison Writings*. SUNY Press, 2005.

Jones, Alison. "Pedagogy by the Oppressed: The Limits of Classroom Dialogue," 8, 1999. https://www.aare.edu.au/data/publications/1999/jon99117.pdf.

Jones, Kenneth, and Tema Okun. *Dismantling Racism: A Workbook for Social Change Groups*. Changework, 2001. https://resourcegeneration.org/wp-content/uploads/2018/01/2016-dRworks-workbook.pdf

Kaba, Mariame. *We Do This 'Til We Free Us: Abolitionist Organizing and Transforming Justice*. Haymarket Books, 2021.

Kaba, Mariame, and Shira Hassan. *Fumbling Towards Repair: A Workbook for Community Accountability Facilitators*. PROJECT NIA, 2019.

Kamola, Isaac. "Guest Blog: Where Does the Bizarre Hysteria About 'Critical Race Theory' Come From? Follow the Money!" Inside Higher Ed, June 3, 2021. https://www.insidehighered.com/blogs/just-visiting/guest-blog-where-does-bizarre-hysteria-about-%E2%80%98critical-race-theory%E2%80%99-come-follow.

King, Mike. "Aggrieved Whiteness: White Identity Politics and Modern American Racial Formation." In *Making Abolitionist Worlds*. Abolition Collective. Philadelphia: Common Notions, 2020.

Kivel, Paul. *Uprooting Racism: How White People Can Work for Racial Justice*. Philadelphia: New Society Publishers, 1996.

Kutz, Christopher. *Complicity: Ethics and Law for a Collective Age*. Cambridge: Cambridge University Press, 2007.

LANDBACK. "LANDBACK." Accessed July 15, 2021. https://landback.org/.

Legault, Lisa, Jennifer Gutsell, and Michael Inzlicht. "Ironic Effects of Antiprejudice Messages: How Motivational Interventions Can Reduce (but Also Increase) Prejudice." *Psychological Science* 22 (November 28, 2011): 1472–77. https://doi.org/10.1177/0956797611427918.

Lepora, Chiara, and Robert E. Goodin. *On Complicity and Compromise*. OUP Oxford, 2013.

Leroux, Daryl. *Distorted Descent*. Winnipeg: University of Manitoba Press, 2019. https://uofmpress.ca/books/detail/distorted-descent.

Lewis, Helen Block. *Shame and Guilt in Neurosis*. 1st edition. International Universities Press, 1971.

Lipsitz, George. *The Possessive Investment in Whiteness: How White People Profit from Identity Politics*. Temple University Press, 2018.

Logan, Erin. "White People Have Gentrified Black Lives Matter. It's a Problem." *Los Angeles Times*, September 4, 2020, sec. Opinion. https://www.latimes.com/opinion/story/2020-09-04/black-lives-matter-white-people-portland-protests-nfl.

López, Ian Haney. *Dog Whistle Politics: How Coded Racial Appeals Have Reinvented Racism and Wrecked the Middle Class*. Oxford University Press, 2013.

Lopez, Ian Haney. *White by Law: The Legal Construction of Race*. NYU Press, 1996.

Lyons, Matthew N. *Insurgent Supremacists: The U.S. Far Right's Challenge to State and Empire*. PM Press, 2018.

Manuel, George, and Michael Posluns. *The Fourth World: An Indian Reality*. University of Minnesota Press, 2019.

Martínez, Ernesto Javier. *On Making Sense: Queer Race Narratives of Intelligibility*. Stanford University Press, 2012.

Massey, Alana. "The White Protestant Roots of American Racism." *The New Republic*, May 26, 2015. https://newrepublic.com/article/121901/white-protestant-roots-american-racism.

May, Larry. *Sharing Responsibility*. University of Chicago Press, 1996.

McCarty, Timothy Wyman. "Insisting on Complicity." *Contemporary Political Theory* 18, no. 1 (2019): 1–21. https://doi.org/10.1057/s41296-018-0257-9.

McGary, Howard. "Morality and Collective Liability." *The Journal of Value Inquiry* 20, no. 2 (June 1, 1986): 157–65. https://doi.org/10.1007/BF00144542.

McGhee, Heather. *The Sum of Us: What Racism Costs Everyone and How We Can Prosper Together*. Random House Publishing Group, 2021.

McKinnon, Rachel. "Allies Behaving Badly: Gaslighting as Epistemic Injustice." In *The Routledge Handbook of Epistemic Injustice*. Routledge, 2017.

Medina, José. *The Epistemology of Resistance: Gender and Racial Oppression, Epistemic Injustice, and Resistant Imaginations*. Oxford: Oxford University Press, 2012.

Mellema, Gregory. *Complicity and Moral Accountability*. Notre Dame: University of Notre Dame Press, 2016. https://muse.jhu.edu/book/45122.

Metzl, Jonathan M. *Dying of Whiteness: How the Politics of Racial Resentment Is Killing America's Heartland*. Basic Books, 2019.

Mills, Charles W. *The Racial Contract*. Cornell University Press, 2014.

———. "White Ignorance." In *Race and Epistemologies of Ignorance*, edited by Nancy Tuana and Shannon Sullivan, 11–38. Albany: SUNY Press, 2012.

Mills, Charles Wade. *Black Rights/White Wrongs: The Critique of Racial Liberalism*. Oxford University Press, 2017.

Mingus, Mia. "Transformative Justice: A Brief Description." *Transform Harm* (blog), January 11, 2019. https://transformharm.org/transformative-justice-a-brief-description/.

Mondon, Aurelien, and Aaron Winter. *Reactionary Democracy: How Racism and the Populist Far Right Became Mainstream*, 2020.

Morrison, Toni. *Playing in the Dark*. Knopf Doubleday Publishing Group, 2007.

Moya, Paula M. L. "What's Identity Got to Do With It? Mobilizing Identities in the Multicultural Classroom." In *Identity Politics Reconsidered*, edited by Linda Martín Alcoff, Michael Hames-García, Satya P. Mohanty, and Paula M. L. Moya, 96–117. The Future of Minority Studies. New York: Palgrave Macmillan US, 2006. https://doi.org/10.1057/9781403983398_7.

Mueller, Jennifer C. "Racial Ideology or Racial Ignorance? An Alternative Theory of Racial Cognition." *Sociological Theory* 38, no. 2 (June 2020): 142–69. https://doi.org/10.1177/0735275120926197.

Murakawa, Naomi, and Katherine Beckett. "The Penology of Racial Innocence: The Erasure of Racism in the Study and Practice of Punishment." *Law & Society Review* 44, no. 3–4 (2010): 695–730.

Narayan, Uma. "Colonialism and Its Others: Considerations On Rights and Care Discourses." *Hypatia* 10, no. 2 (1995): 133–40.

Ngo, Helen. *The Habits of Racism: A Phenomenology of Racism and Racialized Embodiment*. Lexington Books, 2017.

O'Kane, Caitlin. "Nearly a Dozen States Want to Ban Critical Race Theory in Schools," May 20, 2021. https://www.cbsnews.com/news/critical-race-theory-state-bans/.

Olson, Joel. *The Abolition of White Democracy*. University of Minnesota Press, 2004.

Ortega, Mariana. *In-Between: Latina Feminist Phenomenology, Multiplicity, and the Self*. Reprint edition. Albany: State University of New York Press, 2016.

Osnos, Evan. "Can Biden's Center Hold?" *The New Yorker*, n.d.

Pal Singh, Nikhil. "A Note on Race and the Left." *Social Text*, July 31, 2015. https://socialtextjournal.org/a-note-on-race-and-the-left/.

Primoratz, Igor. "Punishment as Language." *Philosophy* 64, no. 248 (1989): 187–205. https://doi.org/10.1017/s0031819100044478.

Probyn, Fiona. "Playing Chicken at the Intersection: The White Critic of Whiteness□." Borderlands E-Journal 13, no. 2 (2004).□□

Rankine, Claudia. *The White Card*. New York: Graywolf Press, 2019. https://www.graywolfpress.org/books/white-card.

Robinson, Cedric J. *Black Marxism: The Making of the Black Radical Tradition*. University of North Carolina Press, 2005.

Rodney, Walter. *How Europe Underdeveloped Africa*. Verso Books, 2018.

Rodogno, Raffaele. "Shame and Guilt in Restorative Justice." *Psychology, Public Policy, and Law* 14, no. 2 (2008): 142–76.

Roediger, David R., and Kendrick C. Babcock Professor of History David R. Roediger. *The Wages of Whiteness: Race and the Making of the American Working Class*. Verso, 1999.

Sakai, J. *Settlers: The Mythology of the White Proletariat from Mayflower to Modern*. PM Press, 2014.

Santos, Boaventura de Sousa. *Epistemologies of the South: Justice Against Epistemicide*. Routledge, 2015.

Schiff, Jacob. "Confronting Political Responsibility: The Problem of Acknowledgment." *Hypatia* 23, no. 3 (2008): 99–117.

Schuller, Kyla. *The Biopolitics of Feeling: Race, Sex, and Science in the Nineteenth Century*. Duke University Press, 2017.

Segrest, Mab. *Memoir of a Race Traitor: Fighting Racism in the American South*, 2019.

Sered, Danielle. *Until We Reckon: Violence, Mass Incarceration, and a Road to Repair*. The New Press, 2019.

Sinha, Manisha. *The Slave's Cause: A History of Abolition*. New Haven: Yale University Press, 2016.

Solomon, Akiba, and Kenrya Rankin. *How We Fight White Supremacy: A Field Guide to Black Resistance*. PublicAffairs, 2019.

Spanierman, Lisa B., and Mary J. Heppner. "Psychosocial Costs of Racism to Whites Scale (PCRW): Construction and Initial Validation." *Journal of Counseling Psychology* 51, no. 2 (2004): 249–62.

Spanierman, Lisa B., Euna Oh, V. Paul Poteat, Anita R. Hund, Vetisha L. McClair, Amanda M. Beer, and Alexis M. Clarke. "White University Students' Responses to Societal Racism: A Qualitative Investigation." *The Counseling Psychologist* 36, no. 6 (August 1, 2008): 839–70. https://doi.org/10.1177/0011000006295589.

Spelman, Elizabeth. "Managing Ignorance." In *Race and Epistemologies of Ignorance*, edited by Nancy Tuana and Shannon Sullivan, 119–31. Albany: SUNY Press, 2012.

Steele. "'White Guilt' and the End of the Civil Rights Era." NPR.org, 2006. https://www.npr.org/templates/story/story.php?storyId=5385701.

Steele, Shelby. *White Guilt: How Blacks and Whites Together Destroyed the Promise of the Civil Rights Era*. HarperCollins, 2009.

Striblen, Cassie. "Guilt, Shame, and Shared Responsibility." *Journal of Social Philosophy* 38 (August 7, 2007): 469–85. https://doi.org/10.1111/j.1467-9833.2007.00392.x.

Sullivan, Shannon. *Good White People: The Problem with Middle-Class White Anti-Racism*. Albany: SUNY Press, 2014.

———. *Revealing Whiteness: The Unconscious Habits of Racial Privilege*. Indiana University Press, 2006.

Sullivan, Shannon, and Nancy Tuana. *Race and Epistemologies of Ignorance*. SUNY Press, 2012.

Swim, Janet, and Deborah Miller. "White Guilt: Its Antecedents and Consequences for Attitudes Toward Affirmative Action." *Personality and Social Psychology Bulletin* 25 (April 1, 1999): 500–514.

Tangney, June Price, and Ronda L. Dearing. *Shame and Guilt*. Guilford Press, 2003.

Tangney, June Price, Jeff Stuewig, and Debra J. Mashek. "Moral Emotions and Moral Behavior." *Annual Review of Psychology* 58 (2007): 345–72. https://doi.org/10.1146/annurev.psych.56.091103.070145.

Tannenbaum, Michael. "Rowan University Drops Emergency Management Official Who Fatally Shot Teen in 1994 | PhillyVoice." Accessed July 6, 2021. https://www.phillyvoice.com/rowan-university-peter-amico-eltarmaine-lt-sanders-shooting-1994-petition/.

Taylor, Keeanga-Yamahtta. *Race for Profit: How Banks and the Real Estate Industry Undermined Black Homeownership*. UNC Press Books, 2019.

Taylor, Paul C. *Race: A Philosophical Introduction*. 1st edition. Cambridge, UK: Malden, MA: Polity, 2013.

———. *Race: A Philosophical Introduction*. John Wiley & Sons, 2013.

Teel, Karen. "Feeling White, Feeling Good: 'Anti-Racist' White Sensibilities." In *White Self-Criticality beyond Anti-Racism: How Does It Feel to Be a White Problem?*, edited by George Yancy, Reprint edition. Lanham Boulder New York London: Lexington Books, 2016.

Todd, Nathan R., and Elizabeth M. Abrams. "White Dialectics: A New Framework for Theory, Research, and Practice With White Students 1Ψ7," 2011. https://doi.org/10.1177/0011000010377665.

Touryalai, Halah. "How Banks Are Getting Richer Off The Poor." Forbes. Accessed June 7, 2021. https://www.forbes.com/sites/halahtouryalai/2012/04/26/how-banks-are-getting-richer-off-the-poor/.

Tracy, Jessica, and Richard Robins. "Appraisal Antecedents of Shame and Guilt: Support for a Theoretical Model." *Personality & Social Psychology Bulletin* 32 (October 1, 2006): 1339–51. https://doi.org/10.1177/0146167206290212.

Vance, J. D. *Hillbilly Elegy: A Memoir of a Family and Culture in Crisis*. HarperCollins, 2018.

Vitale, Alex S. *The End of Policing*. New York: Verso, 2017.

Wang, Jackie. "Against Innocence." *LIES Feminist Journal* 1, no. 1 (2016). https://www.liesjournal.net/volume1-10-againstinnocence.html.

Watson, Lilla. "Contribution to Change: Cooperation out of Conflict Conference: Celebrating Different, Embracing Equality," Keynote, October 25, 2019. https://uniting.church/lilla-watson-let-us-work-together/.

Wekker, Gloria. *White Innocence: Paradoxes of Colonialism and Race*. Duke University Press, 2016.

Welch, Sharon D. *A Feminist Ethic of Risk*. Fortress Press, 1990.

Wiegman, Robyn. *Object Lessons*. Duke University Press, 2012.

Williams, Bernard. *Shame and Necessity*. University of California Press, 2008.

Yancy, George. *Look, A White!: Philosophical Essays on Whiteness*. Temple University Press, 2012.

———. *What White Looks Like: African-American Philosophers on the Whiteness Question*. Psychology Press, 2004.

Young, Damon. "The Term 'White Tears' Is Funny, but What It Often Leads to Isn't." The Root, November 14, 2015. https://www.theroot.com/the-term-white-tears-is-funny-but-what-it-often-lead-1790861731.

Young, Iris Marion. "Responsibility and Global Justice: A Social Connection Model." *Social Philosophy and Policy* 23, no. 1 (January 2006): 102–30. https://doi.org/10.1017/S0265052506060043.

———. *Responsibility for Justice*. Oxford University Press, 2010.

———. "The Five Faces of Oppression." *The Philosophical Forum* XIX, no. 4 (1988): 270–90.

Zhao, Christina. "Coca-Cola, Facing Backlash, Says 'Be Less White' Learning Plan Was About Workplace Inclusion." *Newsweek*, February 21, 2021. https://www.newsweek.com/coca-cola-facing-backlash-says-less-white-learning-plan-was-about-workplace-inclusion-1570875.

Index

About the Author

Eva Boodman is assistant professor of philosophy at Rowan University.

www.ingramcontent.com/pod-product-compliance
Lightning Source LLC
Chambersburg PA
CBHW022321280326
41932CB00010B/1186

9781793639035